USING

COMMON WORSHIP:

Holy Communion

The *Using Common Worship* series
Series editor: Mark Earey

Other titles include:
Funerals – R Anne Horton
Initiation Services – Gilly Myers
Marriage – Stephen Lake

USING
COMMON WORSHIP:
Holy Communion

A Practical Guide to the New Services

Mark Beach

CHURCH HOUSE
PUBLISHING

Church House Publishing
Church House
Great Smith Street
London SW1P 3NZ

ISBN   0 7151 2003 4

Published 2000 by Church House Publishing and *Praxis*

Second impression 2000

Copyright ©   *Praxis 2000*

All rights reserved.Churches have permission to reproduce this publication
in part for the purposes of local discussion,provided the copies include the
above copyright notice and no charge is made for them.Any other
reproduction,storage or transmission of material from this publication by
any means,electronic or mechanical,including photocopying,recording,or
any information storage and retrieval system,requires written permission
which should be sought from the
Copyright and Contracts Administrator,
The Archbishops'Council,
Church House,
Great Smith Street,
London SW1P 3NZ.

Telephone   020 7898 1557
Fax   020 7898 1449
Email   *copyright@c-of-e.org.uk*

Cover design by Silver Fish Creative Marketing

Typeset in 11pt Sabon and 11.5pt Gill Sans by
Pioneer Associates (Graphic) Ltd, Perthshire

Printed by The Cromwell Press Ltd, Trowbridge, Wiltshire

Contents

What is *Praxis*?

Praxis was formed in 1990, sponsored by the Liturgical Commission of the Church of England, the Alcuin Club, and the Group for the Renewal of Worship (GROW). It exists to provide and support liturgical education in the Church of England.

Its aims are:

- to enrich the practice and understanding of worship in the Church of England;

- to serve congregations and clergy in their exploration of the call to worship;

- to provide a forum in which different worshipping traditions can meet and interact.

The name *Praxis* comes from the Greek word for action. It emphasizes our practical concerns and conveys our conviction that worship is a primary expression of the Christian faith.

Praxis runs an annual programme of day conferences and residential workshops around the country, organized either centrally or by *Praxis* regions (informal networks of diocesan liturgical committees).

You can find out more about *Praxis* from our web site: www.sarum.ac.uk/praxis/

For a copy of the *Praxis* programme and details of how to affiliate, contact the *Praxis* office:

Praxis
St Matthew's House
20 Great Peter Street
LONDON
SW1P 2BU
Tel: 020 7222 3704
Fax: 020 7233 0255
Email: praxis@stmw.globalnet.co.uk

Foreword

Those who produced the *Common Worship* services wanted to provide liturgical resources that encourage worshipping communities to take account of the pastoral needs of the congregation and the mission imperative of worship that engages with the surrounding culture.

The synodical process has, rightly, focused on the texts, the structures and the rubrics. But the services will only come to life and reach their potential as living encounters with God in the nitty-gritty of worship in parish churches, hospitals and prison chapels, school halls and other centres of worship. *Praxis* was set up by the Liturgical Commission in partnership with The Group for the Renewal of Worship (GROW) and the Alcuin Club to foster just such a practical approach to liturgy – working at grass roots level to support real churches who are seeking to make their regular worship better. *Praxis* has been running training events and courses to this end for ten years and it is a great step forward to see the combination of deeper undersatanding and better practice coming together in print.

The *Using Common Worship* series is a creative partnership between *Praxis* and Church House Publishing which will help all of us to make the most of *Common Worship*. Each volume bridges the gap between the bare texts and the experience of using those texts in worship. Full of practical advice, backed up with the underlying thinking from members of the Liturgical Commission, these books will be a valuable tool to put alongside the *Common Worship* volumes on the shelves of every worship leader in the Church of England.

✠ *David Sarum*
Chairman of the Liturgical Commission

Acknowledgements

I would like to thank

- Tony Walker, Mike Brock and Jeremy Fletcher for their advice on the pen pictures;

- the people of All Hallows Church, Gedling, for being some of the guinea pigs of liturgical revision;

- my wife Annabel, who has put up with the writing process for longer than either of us imagined;

- Patrick Harris, formerly Bishop of Southwell, for encouraging me to take my interest in pastoral liturgy seriously.

The author and publisher gratefully acknowledge permission to reproduce copyright material in this book. Every effort has been made to trace and contact copyright holders. If there are any inadvertent omissions we apologize to those concerned and undertake to include suitable acknowledgements in all future editions.

Cambridge University Press: Extracts (and adapted extracts) from *The Book of Common Prayer*, the rights in which are vested in the Crown, are reproduced by permission of the Crown's patentee, Cambridge University Press.

The English Language Liturgical Consultation: 'The Lord's Prayer' (modern form) is based on *Praying Together* © ELLC 1988.

SCM-Canterbury Press Norwich: 'We give you thanks and praise' by Alan Griffiths, reproduced from *We Give You Thanks and Praise* (1999) by permission of the publisher.

PART I
Understanding and using Common Worship

Introduction
Jeremy Fletcher

'Here faith would touch and handle things unseen'

Horatius Bonar's words, written in 1855, point towards the
fascination and mystery of Holy Communion in the life of the
Church. In every generation, and in almost every denomination,
the remembrance of Christ's death according to his command has
been a central feature of worship. In this century the influence of
the Parish Communion movement has ensured that Holy
Communion has become the main service for the Church of
England. Bookshelves groan with titles on its theology and
practice, hymnbooks have sections especially devoted to it, and
the testimony of worshippers across the spectrum of faith and
practice is that participating in this sacrament is a key foundation
of their discipleship.

And yet a purely factual summary of a typical Holy Communion
service in an ordinary parish would simply describe people
gathering, singing, listening, standing and sitting, and at a given
point moving forward to eat a small amount of bread and take a
sip of wine before returning to their places and then leaving.
What is it about this activity that challenges and transforms
people, draws them close to God and sends them out with a
mission? The first line of Bonar's hymn gives a clue:

Here, O my Lord, I see thee face to face.

In ways that we cannot explain, we encounter God in the Holy
Communion. Through faith, the mystery of the death of Christ is
made known in bread and wine. As the community gathers
around the table of the Lord, in remembrance and thanksgiving,
so God meets with his people in his word and in a meal shared.
What was then, is now. There is something about the experience
of eating together, challenged and inspired by the word of God,
which transforms an ordinary people and an ordinary activity

into the place where we glimpse heaven and the feast which God has prepared for his people.

No book on the Holy Communion should presume to fathom the depths of what faith touches here. No manual can ever presume to organize the Holy Communion in such a way that it will 'work' according to a particular formula. Nevertheless, attending carefully to how your congregation offers thanksgiving and shares in remembrance can only benefit your community as together you seek to follow in discipleship and be transformed by the God who meets with us in this way. The aim of this book, then, is to aid reflection and make sure our practice only helps and does not hinder people in grasping 'the eternal grace', for here we 'feed upon the Bread of God'; here we drink 'the royal Wine of heaven'.

The rest of this introductory chapter will deal with the genesis of the texts of the Holy Communion in *Common Worship* and will, by its very nature, be somewhat theoretical. Bishop Colin Buchanan is fond of pointing out that the mandatory liturgical material in an hour-long service of Holy Communion takes no more than ten minutes to say. Clearly, the texts are important, but the service only lives when words are brought to life by a worshipping community filling the action with prayer, praise and fellowship. The important part of this book is in the following chapters, which put flesh on the bones of the texts and will concentrate upon Order One (in contemporary language), as being the most widely used.

Holy Communion in *Common Worship*

The Liturgical Commission, when considering the revision of the service of Holy Communion in *The Alternative Service Book 1980* (hereafter ASB), had first to decide whether it should be changed at all. An extensive process of revision from the mid 1960s had seen churches being offered Series 1, Series 2 and Series 3 within eight years of each other. Each brought something new: new texts, a change of shape and finally, in Series 3, a major change of language from 'thou' to 'you'. However, Rite A in the ASB changed Series 3 relatively lightly, which means that many people have been using the same service, by and large, since 1973. The

Commission decided that the changes should be minor, and the Church of England's complicated liturgical revision procedure has now resulted in a text which will feel very familiar to the ASB generation. There are detailed changes, considered below, but the keynote here has been evolution, not revolution.

What is provided?

The Holy Communion in *Common Worship* comprises four Orders. Order One is derived from Rite A, with some changes and many additional resources. Order One in Traditional Language derives from Rite B, but now conforms exactly to Order One in shape. Resources for these services are therefore interchangeable, as long as you mind your language. Order Two is the service of Holy Communion from *The Book of Common Prayer* (hereafter BCP) as it has been commonly adapted, with some material added and rarely-used material omitted; and Order Two in Contemporary Language is the same shape as the BCP service, but in modernized language (and as such is a development of the ASB's 'The Order following the pattern of *The Book of Common Prayer*').

Two founding principles emerge here:

● the importance of shape;

● the bringing together of ancient and modern in one provision.

The importance of shape

The ASB divided its texts into Rites A and B on the basis of their language. *Common Worship* differentiates its services primarily on the basis of their structure. Here CW simply develops and enunciates a pattern of liturgical thinking which has emerged since the ASB. For many people, the ASB acted like another BCP, giving fixed texts in a fixed order. However, a careful study of the rubrics yields much flexibility: alternative texts; permission to create new ones ('in these or other suitable words'); and options to omit or move others. Though the service structure also gained a degree of flexibility, it was the permission to insert new texts into the existing structure which marked a revolution in the liturgical provision for the Church of England.

Publications such as *Lent, Holy Week, Easter* (1984), *The Promise of His Glory* (1991) and *Patterns for Worship* (1995) developed this 'directory approach', providing seasonal and thematic resources which could be placed into an underlying service structure. That *A Service of the Word* (1994) also allowed the very structure of a non-eucharistic service to gain flexibility, depending upon circumstance, simply reinforces the point that contemporary worship in the Church of England starts with shape and only then moves on to text. The service of Holy Communion in *Common Worship* is therefore based on two underlying structures: the modern 'Western' shape for Order One, and the BCP shape for Order Two. Though this does not signify the end of the battle for an appropriate sacred language, a battle which dogged the Church of England throughout the 1970s and beyond, it does make an important point. Where once we had prayer in common because we used the same *texts*, we can still have prayer in common because the underlying *structures* of the service are familiar to us.

Ancient and modern

To many people the ASB seemed brash in its modernizing of the liturgy. Even though it introduced rich resources and some wonderful texts to the Church ('Father of all . . .', the post communion prayer, was newly written for Series 3), it had very few echoes of the riches of *The Book of Common Prayer*. Since its main services contained no Prayer Book texts, many congregations felt that the tradition which had nurtured them had been consigned to the history books. The enduring nature of the Prayer Book, and a reassessment of the 'world-view' of the ASB, has meant that in the *Common Worship* main volume not only will Prayer Book services be included (amended to reflect the way the Prayer Book has been used), but also Prayer Book texts will be found within the resources for contemporary language services. There has also been a specific policy to create new texts with Prayer Book resonance, not in a desire to get back to a golden age, but in order to recognize that we are formed by our traditions and that the dynamic of Anglicanism is to build on tradition rather than reject it out of hand.

Common Worship is the first official Church of England publication to include services from the Prayer Book as well as newly written ones. The BCP services are not strictly identical to those found in *The Book of Common Prayer*, because they are an attempt to print them as congregations normally use them. Texts such as the Summary of the Law and Agnus Dei are included, and the exhortations are removed (though one is in the Supplementary Texts). Time will tell if the inclusion of these services in the *Common Worship* main volume will introduce them to a new set of worshippers and mark a revival in their use!

Theological and doctrinal issues: Order One

Though it is important to acknowledge the variety of provision for the Holy Communion in *Common Worship*, the most widely used service will be Order One. It is a development of Rite A, itself the most widespread order for Communion in the Church of England. In discussing specific issues of theology, doctrine and structure in the rest of this chapter, and in the discussion of the practical use of the Communion service, Order One will be in mind.

The Creed

Because Holy Communion in *Common Worship* is an evolution of the ASB Eucharist, there are few new areas which have caused great theological or doctrinal controversy. Perhaps of greatest weight is the reference to the Incarnation in the Nicene Creed, where the ASB text 'by the power of the Holy Spirit he became incarnate of the Virgin Mary' has been changed. After much debate, the translation agreed by ELLC (the English Language Liturgical Consultation, an international body concerned with agreeing the translation of texts held in common by English-speaking churches) was adopted with one exception. Where ELLC had 'was incarnate *of* the Holy Spirit and the Virgin Mary', the version finally approved now reads '*from* the Holy Spirit and the Virgin Mary'. Synod debates made clear that the doctrine of the Incarnation itself was never in question, but that it was important to find a translation of the Greek text of the creed which would express this most clearly. Some felt that different prepositions (*'by* the Holy Spirit *of* the Virgin Mary') would communicate the distinctive roles within the Incarnation of Christ. The final translation acknowledges that the Greek has only one preposition and that the translation 'from' brings out the dynamic of the Incarnation better than 'of'. It has to be said that a majority of Synod members initially favoured 'of', but enough people were unhappy with it for 'from' to win the day eventually.

It should also be noted that the Nicene Creed in *Common Worship* also departs from ELLC in the next line. Where ELLC reads 'and became truly human', CW has the familiar 'and was made man'. Though the Church of England has clear guidelines for gender-inclusive language (detailed in *Making Women Visible*, 1989) it was felt that 'human' or 'fully' or 'truly human' were unsatisfactory either for stylistic reasons or because of resonances of fallibility ('he's only human'). The Church of England's solution to the *filioque* debate (the ancient controversy about whether the Holy Spirit proceeds from the Father and the Son, or the Father alone) is to print the ecumenically-agreed creed without the *filioque* clause in the Creeds section of the *Common Worship* main volume, for use on 'suitable ecumenical occasions'.

Confession

The Holy Communion in *Common Worship* contains two confession prayers as alternatives in the main text. Though the ASB did provide three prayers of confession, only one of these was in the main text, the others being in an appendix. Order One has six confessions in the Supplementary Texts, but also places a choice in the main text because the two confessions reflect different theological standpoints. During the revision process strong representations were made that sin could only be committed against God, not against human beings. Only in the later years of this century has the praying tradition of the Church of England referred to sin 'against our fellow men', and some felt that, though we should acknowledge the ways in which we have hurt other people, we should only speak of sin as that which refers to God. The alternative confession included in the main text speaks of our failure to love God and love our neighbour, but uses the word sin only in relation to God. The prayer has resonances of the Summary of the Law and the prophet Micah, and derives from Series 2 Morning and Evening Prayer. It is a welcome addition to our mainstream acts of worship.

Eucharistic prayer

Veterans of the liturgical debates of recent years will know that controversy has centred around the nature of the words 'offering' and 'sacrifice'. Neither of these areas has been much at issue for CW, and the theological debate has been concentrated around the *epiclesis*: the invocation of the Holy Spirit upon the action of the Holy Communion in the prayer of thanksgiving. The line held here is that the Holy Spirit is invoked on the whole of the assembly and action, including the elements of bread and wine, so that in communion the bread and wine may be to us the body and blood of Christ. At no point here is the Spirit asked to be specifically and locally present upon the elements, and an attempt to ask the Spirit to be sent 'upon these gifts' was repelled during debate. The phrases found in the different eucharistic prayers reflect the Spirit's work upon the elements of bread and wine, but do not ask for this specifically.

The advantage of a variety of eucharistic prayers is that the breadth of eucharistic doctrine does not have to be encapsulated in one prayer alone. This is well illustrated in the related issue about the *epiclesis*: its position in the prayer. Different traditions have placed the *epiclesis* before or after the words of institution, or sometimes in both places, and elements of those traditions are represented in the eight prayers provided in Order One. This is a specific change from the ASB, which provided four prayers which conformed to the same basic structure. However, *Common Worship* has followed the ASB's general lead in offering a variety of prayers in order to open up the possibilities of the eucharistic prayer and widen the range of biblical imagery, symbolism and allusion.

CW Prayer A is a conflation of the ASB's Prayers 1 and 2. Prayer B is a gentle reworking of ASB's Prayer 3, and Prayer C of ASB's Prayer 4. The new prayers are Prayers D to H. Prayer D is full of concrete imagery and, like Prayer E, is deliberately short. Prayer E provides many longer prefaces to be used in seasons. Prayer F is a significant change, giving the Church of England an 'Eastern' shape prayer whose first section focuses on God the Father, turns to God the Son in the narrative of institution and ends with a call to God the Holy Spirit to come upon the assembly. Prayer G restores some of the kingdom banquet imagery lost from the old Prayer 2 and adds some memorable phrases such as 'the silent music of your praise'. All these prayers contain acclamations and responses for the congregation, giving them more of a voice in what has been largely a priestly prayer.

The most radical prayer is Prayer H, not for its theology but for its nature. Synod, at a late stage, was asked for a prayer in which the congregation could not only make their acclamations, but also speak words which moved the sense of the prayer along. Many congregations had been joining in paragraphs of existing prayers, but it was felt that a new prayer was needed. Though not unique in the Anglican Communion (Kenya has a well-known example), this is a first for the Church of England and time will tell if congregations both take to it and commit their sections to memory so as to join in the drama rather than have their heads buried in a book.

The increasing participation of congregations in the eucharistic prayer does have implications, I believe, for their physical participation in the rite. Cranmer expected the congregation to gather round the table for the narrative of institution, before receiving straight away. Prayer H (and the other prayers to a greater or lesser extent) imply participation in the prayer: these are not for private use with a distant priest whose back is to the congregation. At least, there should be good sight-lines, so that all the worshippers in the assembly can see both table and president, but I wonder whether Cranmer's ideal of gathering around the table might not be a good one to aim at where congregation and priest join in dialogue to celebrate and proclaim Christ's death for the world.

Other doctrinal points

The question of offering, which was not really a theological issue in the eucharistic prayer, does arise in the section called

Preparation of the Table and Taking of the Bread and Wine. The ASB had a prayer derived from 2 Chronicles which really referred to money ('Yours Lord . . .') but was often used as a prayer over the gifts of bread and wine which had been placed on the table at this point. CW gives a set of rubrics which outline a preferred order and provides twelve 'Prayers at the Preparation of the Table' in the Supplementary Texts. Some of these refer directly to money, some more generally to the whole of the action of the section and some specifically to bread and wine. The word 'offer' is found in these prayers, but used in such a way as to distance us from any sense that we can offer God anything in our worship other than our response to God's offering of Christ to us. The Offertory is a part of the service where churches have developed all sorts of elaborate rituals which might even eclipse the great drama of the eucharistic prayer, and inadvertently send out all sorts of wrong signals about the glorification of money or the splendour of our own offering. The change to Order One gives churches the opportunity to look carefully at their practice at this point.

Some other significant, though detailed, changes include:

- new gospel responses which address Christ directly ('Glory to you, O Lord'; 'Praise to you, O Christ');

- the omission of the word 'him' from the opening dialogue of the eucharistic prayer ('It is right to give thanks and praise') as being a more faithful translation of the original, which did not refer to God at all – 'it is meet and right so to do' is a good version!

- the insertion by rubric of a time of silent prayer before the Collect;

- the omission of scriptural sentences from the opening of the service and the post communion section; these were a late addition to the ASB and a note allows their inclusion, but there is no reference to them in the main text.

Underlying principles

Worshippers will always judge any service which replaces a familiar one by what has changed, and often it is the small changes which irritate and draw disproportionate attention to themselves. Holy Communion in *Common Worship* has some of these, but it is the development of some deeper principles which is of most interest here. Five underlying principles emerge, which have their roots in the ASB and its predecessors, but which find greater expression in *Common Worship*. They are:

- dependence on a deep structure;
- use of a clean text;
- careful nomenclature for titles and sections;
- development of distinct roles in the Liturgy;
- increasing variety of resources.

Deep structure

Common Worship will eventually consist of an almost unlimited collection of services, published in a number of volumes and in electronic form, with the possibility of endless variations as different resources are used. This is a long way from the one-volume provision of *The Book of Common Prayer*, with its fixed order and little seasonal variation. This leaves CW open to the accusation that the worship is anything but 'common', because two neighbouring churches will almost certainly pick radically differing patterns for their worship from what is on offer. Even in the Holy Communion, the meal which unites us, there will be two shapes, each with linguistic variants, and up to eight eucharistic prayers in Order One alone, eight confessions and so on. For some this is a nightmare, especially those who travel from church to church rather than staying in one place.

In considering this, it is essential to get the history right. Even though the BCP was a text held in common by the Church of England, its use was incredibly different from church to church. Some altered its order, and all churches applied their local 'feel' in the choice of hymns and the simplicity or elaboration of their ritual. From the late 1800s churches also had permission to provide other services on a Sunday as long as they also fulfilled their obligations to have Holy Communion and Morning and Evening Prayer. The reality of worship across the Church of England is that there has always been a variety of both texts and practice, held together more often by the way our worship has been conducted and its common features. *Common Worship* (following the ASB) simply offers good resources for local churches to be Anglican where they are, enabling local differences to develop within broad boundaries of practice, with essential texts that are doctrinally sound.

It is not now possible to guarantee that if you go to Holy Communion in a new church one Sunday you will know all the texts which will be used. However, it is more than likely that you will recognize the 'feel' of the service, because Anglican worship has always been a way of doing things as well as a collection of texts. There will be an underlying shape to the service, giving a security where the texts may be unfamiliar. This shape and structure has a number of levels. On the surface there will be the particular mix of ingredients for that Sunday, with the prayers of penitence in one position, the Liturgy of the Word including readings and a psalm, and specific choices for the Confession, Prayer of Humble Access and Eucharistic Prayer, together with a choice of hymns and the material proper to the day (such as the Collect).

Underneath this surface structure for that specific service is the order from which it derives, in this case Order One. The order is capable of superficial variation and allows material to be inserted for each Sunday, but it retains its overall shape, so that its basic pattern is recognizable even though the surface elements may change. Underneath the order, however, is the deep structure of corporate worship, which is now more recognizable in the shape of the services in *Common Worship* and which has a strong pastoral element. This deep structure might best be described as Gathering, Transformation and Mission.

Gathering includes elements of welcome, introduction, acknowledgement of the purpose of the service, preparation and penitence. Transformation comes through our meeting with God in the proclamation of the word and the sacrament of communion. Simply put, we should not leave the place of worship as the same people who entered it. As individuals we will have encountered the forgiveness and restoration promised by God and been included in the life of the Trinity and the worship of heaven. We will have offered the reality of our lives in penitence, thanksgiving and intercession. As a community we will have been transformed into the kingdom people of God around the table which is a foretaste of the heavenly banquet.

Though this might not be your actual experience Sunday by Sunday, it is all a part of the mystery of Holy Communion which we are offered, and for which we should strive. How can we not be changed if the death of Christ for the world and for us has been proclaimed in word and sacrament? Mission follows naturally. Having met with God and been transformed into the people of the kingdom, we are sent into the world 'to love and serve the Lord'. Eucharist sends us out.

In any act of worship this deep structure will have its influence and must be allowed to speak. There is nothing worse than being sent out at the dismissal ('Go in peace') and then being told to stay where you are for the notices. Neither should there be a confusion of beginnings, with informal and formal welcomes and introductions all spread around a hymn and procession. For this reason the text of Order One as printed is clear about order (informal welcomes come after the Greeting, for example) and deliberately simple in structure, putting a variety of resources in an appendix away from the main text. Those producing their own texts might well follow this lead: offer a simple and clear structure and order, and insert your resources week by week. Worship Sunday by Sunday can then begin to breathe and regular worshippers can feel some sense of order even as everything changes around them. And what could be better for the newcomer than a clear text with an obvious shape?

Clean text

Common Worship will be published in a variety of formats. Uniquely in the Church of England, publication will be simultaneous as a book, disk, computer program and on the Internet. In all of these the key criteria will be useability and simplicity of presentation. In the book, for example, the principle has been that only essential congregational words are printed in the main text, with other seasonal or occasional resources contained in the Supplementary Texts. There may be over 150 pages in the Communion section, but only a fraction of them are essential for the regular worshipper and these are contained at the front of each order to save much page turning.

Clearly, communications technology is now so cheap and widespread that only some churches will buy the complete *Common Worship* main volume for every member of their congregation; many will print their own versions as one-off pamphlets, or even Sunday by Sunday. Others will project the words, or buy separate booklets, perhaps having a few copies of the main volume for reference. Where churches print locally, the underlying principles of simplicity and ease of use must be borne in mind. The point is that the texts should help, not hinder, and the main volume in *Common Worship* will act as an example of best practice in this regard.

However, even here there will be rubrics and texts which are essential for the rite, but which local congregations may not need to see Sunday by Sunday. Churches will have to take their own decisions as to what to include, balancing ease of use with the teaching function that service books also provide. It is possible to give too little and, as the essentials for worship are provided each week, individual worshippers might be encouraged to buy the main volume for themselves and commit the service to memory or explore the riches of the provision at greater leisure (rather than during the sermon like choirboys of old!).

What's in a name? Titles and section headings

Language has a symbolic as well as a practical function. Only this can explain the discussions in the General Synod over words in this service which will never actually be used by worshippers Sunday by Sunday. One such debate was about the title of the service, with 'The Eucharist' being the preferred option initially. Anglican tradition has always given more than one title to the service. In 1549 Cranmer called it 'The Supper of the Lord and The Holy Communion, Commonly Called The Mass', with prominence given to 'The Holy Communion'. The ASB called it 'The Order for Holy Communion, also called The Eucharist, and the Lord's Supper', and again gave priority to 'Holy Communion'. *Common Worship* calls it 'The Order for the Celebration of **Holy Communion** also called **The Eucharist** and **The Lord's Supper**', giving priority again to 'Holy Communion', but adding a note of celebration to mark the fact that the service is celebrated by all the people of God.

The debate over titles was important, in that it became clear that no one title would do. 'The Eucharist' seemed too 'catholic' for some, whilst being a good liturgical shorthand for others, attractive as the title used in ecumenical discourse and speaking of thanksgiving as the main action of the rite. 'Holy Communion' draws attention to the participation of the people of God in the service and their meeting with God in receiving consecrated bread and wine. 'The Lord's Supper' is a reminder of the derivation of this meal from the Last Supper and brings resonances of the Passover meal and the banquet of the redeemed in heaven at the end of time. Each church will no doubt settle for one title on its noticeboards and service sheets, but this variety of title serves to prevent us from narrowing the focus of the service too much.

A change has also been made in one of the headings in the service, which again will not be said by any worshipper but nevertheless sends important signals. The ASB spoke of the *Ministry* of the Word, and the *Ministry* of the Sacrament. *Common Worship* now has the *Liturgy* of the Word and the *Liturgy* of the Sacrament. This significant change (first made in the *Common Worship* Initiation Services) comes because the word 'ministry' has now come to refer quite specifically to the action of ministers in exercising their ministry. The proclamation of the word and the sharing of the sacrament in Communion cannot be confined simply to ministerial actions: the CW Holy Communion is clear that all are involved in proclaiming and receiving the word and sharing in the sacrament. The word liturgy originally derives from the Greek for 'work of the people', and it was felt that it had now been stripped of any academic or elitist overtones. The liturgy is something in which the whole gathering takes part.

Roles in the liturgy

Notes are not exactly the most riveting part of any liturgy and the majority of worshippers will never choose to read them. Though this is understandable, they often contain great riches and, at a practical level, act like the hidden codes in computer programs, unseen but vital. *Common Worship* has taken the decision to print the notes at the back of each service, but in the Holy Communion this policy has been changed to allow certain key notes to be given prominence. Chief among these is a note on ministries, which marks a change of feel from the ASB. The note begins by saying, 'Holy Communion is celebrated by the whole people of God gathered for worship', and affirms the fact that all worshippers have their part to play in the liturgy. Specific roles are given to the deacon and priest (and to the bishop as chief minister of the liturgy when present), but these roles only find their place within the whole act of worship. *Common Worship* is clear that worship is offered by all, and the printing, structure and feel of the text are designed to aid this participation. A church community which takes the note on ministries seriously will find itself unearthing depths of fellowship and worship previously unplumbed and untapped.

Variety of resources

At first sight, the eucharistic provision in *Common Worship* will seem dizzyingly complex. First you must choose one of two shapes, and then a contemporary or traditional language option. If you choose Order One, there are two Introductions, two Confessions (with six more in the Supplementary Texts), no set form of intercession (but five in the Supplementary Texts), any number of seasonal introductions to the Peace, eight eucharistic prayers and so on. Succeeding chapters in this book will give you a way through Order One, but the problem here is rather like opening the instruction manual for a washing machine. Though there are any number of possibilities on offer, in the end you will plump for the programme which suits your needs and consult the manual if something new arises. Order One is much like the ASB in its structure and feel, and if handled carefully the extra resources only embellish and never obscure it.

Given the desire for a 'clean' text, the use of alternatives in the main text has been kept to a minimum. Again, there have been issues about the symbolic placing of important texts in positions of prominence. The Ten Commandments are clearly a central text for Christian belief and practice, and some felt that they should be found in the main text in Order One, as they are in Order Two. However, Sunday by Sunday, worship leaders have tended to use the Commandments only infrequently, and in *Common Worship* they are included in the Supplementary Texts (in a number of forms) so that they can be used powerfully as part of the prayers of penitence (in Advent and Lent, for example) yet not be conspicuous by their lack of use the rest of the time.

This decision was not without its opponents, and a creative solution has been worked out which adds a new dimension to the Holy Communion for the Church of England. There is now a 'Penitential Introduction to the Eucharist', printed immediately before Order One. It can be used either by individual worshippers as part of their personal preparation, or as a separate penitential service by a congregation, or as part of the penitential section in the Communion itself. The Commandments are printed here and so have a prominent place before the service, as well as being in the resource material. This new introduction thus adds to the depth and breadth of the service, without placing material in the main text which might be passed over on a regular basis; careful planning by the leader of worship will add greatly to the way worshippers prepare for the service itself.

Conclusion: Order, order

In providing these texts for use by the Church of England, the Liturgical Commission and the General Synod have had to concentrate on the texts and their doctrinal and linguistic content. These services have been designed to be used in good faith by any Anglican church, in that there are no 'party' texts – everyone should be able to use every text, though they may not choose to do so. The process has not just been about words, however. In the minds of all the participants in the process has been the *action* of the liturgy, and the rubrics and notes are there to help worshippers make the words of the service come alive. Worship is a mysterious interaction between humanity both fallen and redeemed and God both immanent and transcendent. At its centre is Jesus Christ, humanity offered to God and God offered to us. If these services, and this book, serve to aid that interaction and enable us to 'touch and handle things unseen', then something worthwhile will have happened. May God make it so.

1 Setting the scene

As the new generation of worship material emerges into the light of day in the Church of England, clergy, lay worship leaders and PCCs will face a bewildering array of choices.

- How do we introduce *Common Worship* into our church?

- Shall we make use of the new variety that is included in the service or continue to use the same material each week?

- How can we use the new material as an opportunity for teaching on the meaning of Holy Communion?

In the following pages I will address these issues and many others in an attempt to make the transition to *Common Worship* as smooth as possible. It is my hope that through this essentially practical and pastoral book, clergy and those with a responsibility for the planning and leading of worship will be encouraged to look carefully at their current practice and at the opportunities provided by *Common Worship*.

The book will, in many places, make reference to both *The Book of Common Prayer* (or BCP) and *The Alternative Service Book 1980* (or ASB). Both these books are an important part of the process by which we have arrived at *Common Worship*, and they allow us to see how the new texts may be used from a context with which we are familiar.

Appropriate choices

Throughout this book you will find references to making appropriate choices, to the extent that you might tire of reading the words! The ASB offered choice to the planner and leader of worship, but often the choices were hidden away, so that only the devoted liturgist could discover them. *Common Worship* brings the choices out into the open. You will still need to look carefully to find the choices, but with the help of this book their use will be clear.

Four pen pictures

In order to give some examples from the different traditions of the Church and to put some flesh on the dry bones of the texts, I have created four sample parishes which I will use as examples throughout. These four pictures are based on a composite of real life; as such, they do not always represent best practice!

> **St Matthew's**
>
> Twenty years ago, the parish of St Matthew's was open fields. Now it is a large, middle-class, residential area. The focal point of the modern church building is the altar, expressing the centrality of Holy Communion to the congregation.
>
> Matty's, the children's church, is a thriving part of the church. They use the *Partners in Learning* material, recognizing the importance of the younger members of the congregation following the same pattern of readings as those who meet in church. Children are admitted to Holy Communion on the basis of their baptism.
>
> The Parish Profile written during a recent vacancy described the church as 'Modern Catholic'. Incense is used at festivals and on saints' days and the liturgy has a relaxed formality. There is a large robed choir which sings anything from Monteverdi to Graham Kendrick. Christmas is known as the 'Rutter-tide festival'!
>
> They use seasonal booklets for the Parish Eucharist, drawn from *Common Worship* Order One, *Enriching the Christian Year* and other sources.
>
> Order Two in traditional language is used for the 8 a.m. said Holy Communion which attracts a steady congregation of about 25. The similarities to *The Book of Common Prayer* are such that this has met with little or no opposition. This arrangement was adopted when *Common Worship* was published because the PCC wanted all the services to be using *Calendar, Lectionary and Collects* as the source of readings.

The new incumbent is a member of the Diocesan Liturgical Committee and has experience of using the *Common Worship* services in her previous parish, which was one of the 'experimental parishes' authorized to try out the *Common Worship* material as it was written.

St Mark's

St Mark's is a large, Victorian building set in a deprived urban area. The congregation of 60 struggles to maintain the building but remains committed to worshipping and witnessing in the community. They were encouraged by the *Faith in the City* report, but more than ten years on wonder what their priorities should be now.

Their worship is predominantly eucharistic, although, as they seek to relate to their community, they would accept no party label. The Parish Communion is the main service each week and on one Sunday a month it is in the evening. Lay participation is actively encouraged.

The vicar has not given time to being at the forefront of liturgical change, and prior to the publication of *Common Worship* had not paid much attention to liturgy. However, a Deanery Chapter meeting led by a member of the Diocesan Liturgical Committee in 1999 encouraged him to look more carefully at the material he was using in worship.

The church boasts a fine organ, but there is a shortage of people who can play it. Often the only music available is the vicar's guitar.

The Book of Common Prayer is used for evensong once a month.

St Luke's

Since the early 1980s, St Luke's has been a major charismatic/evangelical church, attracting its congregation from a wide area. Holy Communion is held every Sunday but at different times of the day. On one Sunday each month it is the main service.

The major emphases within the church are on the exercise of spiritual gifts within the congregation, teaching and evangelism. Worship is carefully planned with these goals in mind. Lay participation is very widespread.

The church uses the 'little red' ASB separates, with little seasonal or other variety. There is a time of ministry for healing and prayer in every service, led by lay people. Many members of the congregation take part in preaching, which takes a variety of forms from a formal didactic model to the way-out!

The music is of a high standard, with a group consisting of keyboard and a variety of instrumentalists who practise together regularly. They are keen to explore the latest worship music and to teach the congregation new songs.

The lectionary is rarely used, but the church eldership plans teaching series around particular books of the Bible or themes. The children's work follows Scripture Union material, with large groups meeting during the morning service.

St John's

Set in a small village, St John's is a small, medieval building. It is part of a multi-parish benefice. St John's is at its busiest at festivals, especially Harvest and Christmas. There are, in effect, four congregations according to the monthly pattern of worship in the church.

On two Sundays each month the service is Morning Prayer from the ASB; one Sunday sees Holy Communion from the BCP. The busiest service is the monthly Family Service but many of the congregation only attend on that Sunday.

The vicar and lay leaders are keen to introduce eucharistic worship to this new congregation, whom they see as the future of the church. In order to achieve this they have a special order of service, which uses popular songs in place of the Gloria and Sanctus.

The PCC decided to adopt *Calendar, Lectionary and Collects* on Advent Sunday in 1997 and has welcomed this new approach to reading the Bible in worship. The small but lively children's groups have been using *Living Stones* since then.

Shape and language

The shape of *Common Worship*: Order One and Order Two

Common Worship contains two Orders for the Holy Communion. Order One has the shape of the ASB, the modern Western shape, while Order Two follows the order of *The Book of Common Prayer* 'as used'.

'As used' is a recognition of the fact that the Communion service in *The Book of Common Prayer* is seldom used just as you find it in the Prayer Book. Instead, it is used with what the General Synod Revision Committee called 'customary variations'. For the details behind these changes see Chapter 6.

The language of *Common Worship*: traditional and contemporary

Both Order One (ASB shape) and Order Two (BCP 'as used') appear in two forms. One of these is in contemporary language and the other in traditional language. This is a development from the ASB that combines Rites A and B and 'The Order following the pattern of the Book of Common Prayer' of the ASB. For the detail of these changes see Chapter 6.

	Modern Western (ASB) shape (ecumenical)	**BCP shape**
Traditional language	Order One (Traditional)	Order Two
Contemporary language	Order One	Order Two (Contemporary)

23

It should also be noted that the traditional version of texts may be used in Order One (see Order One, note 2, p. 330). In particular this applies to the Lord's Prayer, which is printed in two versions, as below:

As our Saviour taught us, so we pray

All **Our Father in heaven,
hallowed be your name,
your kingdom come,
your will be done,
on earth as in heaven.
Give us today our daily bread.
Forgive us our sins
as we forgive those who sin against us.
Lead us not into temptation
but deliver us from evil.
For the kingdom, the power,
and the glory are yours
now and for ever.
Amen.**

(or)

Let us pray with confidence as our Saviour has taught us

All **Our Father, who art in heaven,
hallowed be thy name;
thy kingdom come;
thy will be done;
on earth as it is in heaven.
Give us this day our daily bread.
And forgive us our trespasses,
as we forgive those who trespass against us.
And lead us not into temptation;
but deliver us from evil.
For thine is the kingdom,
the power and the glory,
for ever and ever.
Amen.**

What's new in *Common Worship*?

The truth is that not very much of the core material in the *Common Worship* Holy Communion has changed, especially in Order One. This is because the Liturgical Commission took the view that so much of the energy spent on the creation of the ASB, through Series 1, 2 and 3, was on the eucharistic material that for the most part congregations are happy with the existing material. However, the appearance of *Common Worship* does provide us with a valuable opportunity to re-assess the way in which we celebrate Holy Communion in our churches.

The table overleaf shows how various parts of the service have changed from *The Book of Common Prayer* through the ASB to *Common Worship* Order One.

	BCP/1928 *Traditional language*	**ASB Rite A** *Contemporary language*	**CW Order One** *Both traditional language and contemporary language*
Gathering and Preparation			
Greeting	Lord's Prayer Collect for Purity	Greeting and Sentence Collect for Purity	Fuller greeting No sentence Collect for Purity
Penitential Rite	Before Prayer of Consecration	Summary of the Law Prayers of Penitence May be used later in service	Material for use in preparing for worship Wider variety of penitential material available Normally at the start of the service

The position of the prayers of penitence will influence their nature. At the start of the service penitence is in preparation for the whole service. Coming between the Liturgies of Word and Sacrament it serves as confession in the light of having heard the word.

Liturgy of the Word			
Bible Readings	Epistle and Gospel	Three readings and Psalm: Thematic	Three readings and Psalm: Semi-continuous
Prayers of Intercession	Prayer for the Church Militant	Prayers of Intercession: Three forms provided	Prayers of Intercession: Wider variety available, including Collect ending for intercessions

The main text of *Common Worship* contains only the barest bones of Prayers of Intercession: subject headings and default responses. The Supplementary Texts contain five different texts and a selection of different responses and Collect endings.

Penitential Rite	Only position	If not used earlier. May include the Comfortable Words. May be followed by Prayer of Humble Access	Penitential material may be used here, especially in appropriate seasons, but not printed here in the texts

Liturgy of the Sacrament

Prayer of Humble Access	Before Prayer of Consecration	Before the Peace	Immediately before Communion

The Prayer of Humble Access is seen in *Common Worship* as a response to the invitation to Communion, 'Draw near with faith . . .' Both the BCP form ('We do not presume . . .'), in both modern and traditional language, and the ASB contemporary form are given ('Most merciful Lord . . .'). Both are for congregational use.

Prayer after Communion

Prayer after Communion	Either prayer of Oblation or of Thanksgiving	An appropriate sentence may be said. Two prayers provided (one congregational)	Post Communion from *Common Worship:* Calendar, Lectionary and Collects; two further prayers provided, both congregational

One or two prayers may be used. If two are used, one should be presidential and should normally come from the *Calendar, Lectionary and Collects* provision for the day. The prayer 'Father of all . . .' is printed as a congregational text.

Seasonal provisions

A further area in which *Common Worship* differs from both the BCP and the ASB is the extensive provision for various seasons. In an appendix for both Order One and Order Two there is a selection of texts as follows:

- *Invitation to Confession*: with a scriptural base looking towards confession.

- *Gospel Acclamation*: scriptural sentences surrounded by Alleluias. During Lent this is 'Praise to you, O Christ, King of eternal glory'.

- *Introduction to the Peace*: similar to ASB, but with a wider selection of choices both for the seasons and for general use.

- *Eucharistic Preface*: in both contemporary and traditional language. Similar to ASB, but with new extended prefaces.

- *Blessing*: similar to ASB, with wider selection of choices.

The following seasons and principal holy days are provided for in this way:

- The First Sunday of Advent until Christmas Eve

- Christmas Day until the Eve of the Epiphany

- Epiphany until the Eve of the Presentation

- The Presentation of Christ in the Temple

- Ash Wednesday until the Saturday after the Fourth Sunday in Lent

- The Annunciation of Our Lord (with a note that if the Annunciation falls in Eastertide the provision for Christmas Day is used)

- Fifth Sunday of Lent (Passion Sunday) until the Wednesday of Holy Week

- Maundy Thursday

- Easter Day until the Eve of the Ascension

- Ascension Day

- The day after Ascension Day until the day of Pentecost

- Trinity Sunday

- All Saints' Day

- The day after All Saints' Day until the day before the First Sunday of Advent

- Saints' days.

In this way, seasonal material is gathered into one place for each season rather than being laid out according to the point in the service at which it is to be used.

Using the default settings

To borrow an illustration from the computer world, it is all too easy to use only the default settings. That is what will happen if you only use the texts contained within the main part of the book. By doing this, you reduce considerably the power of the computer to produce attractive, easily readable text.

In liturgical terms, you will miss out on the wide variety of material provided as options for seasonal use or to emphasize different parts of the service. Much of the content of this book will concern the use of this material.

Many churches have been happy to use one set of texts for Holy Communion and their default setting has been 'the little red book'. It has been so much easier to simply hand out the books each week and go straight through, starting on page 119! This will not be possible in *Common Worship* because some parts of the service do not have a default setting in the main text. For example, at the Peace the text says simply:

> *The president may introduce the Peace with a suitable sentence, and then says*

However, it would still be easy to fall into the trap of using the familiar introductions to the Peace and not benefiting from the wide selection provided in the seasonal material and the Supplementary Texts.

In their use of the ASB some churches will have varied the Eucharistic Prayer, but this is often done on a weekly rotation rather than by looking at a seasonal use of the prayers or using prayers according to the congregation at a particular service.

Common Worship provides us with a new challenge. It is the challenge to change the defaults and use the variety that is available to us. Modern computer technology, with a basic word processor or desktop publishing program, can make variety relatively simple.

For example:

• During Lent use might be made of the Ten Commandments as an extended penitential section.

• A series of seasonal booklets might be printed using the provision in *Common Worship* or from *Enriching the Christian Year* (SPCK/Alcuin Club, 1993). The full range of seasonal material for *Common Worship* will be published as a separate book, likely to be called *Times and Seasons*. This is expected to be available in 2003.

But a note of caution should be sounded:

The choices that are opened up to the planners and leaders of worship can provide stimulating variety in worship. However, if the choice is used without careful thought and planning the result is more likely to be spiritual indigestion!

For help in creating your own service booklets, see Mark Earey's useful book, *Producing Your Own Orders of Service* (*Praxis*/CHP, 2000).

Things that might trip you up

There are a few other, more minor, changes that need to be pointed out to the unsuspecting. For example:

• *Introduction to the Gospel reading*

Hear the Gospel of our Lord Jesus Christ according to N.
All **Glory to you, O Lord.**

This change is a return to the phrase used in earlier modern rites (Series 1), 'Glory be to thee, O Lord'. The significance of the change is to address the response to the Gospel directly to Christ, rather than indirectly as in the ASB's 'Glory to Christ our Saviour'. A similar change is made to the response after the Gospel reading.

- *The Sursum Corda*

> Let us give thanks to the Lord our God.
> *All* **It is right to give thanks and praise.**

Not 'It is right to give *him* thanks and praise'.

- *Prayer of Humble Access*

> **that our sinful bodies may be made clean by his body
> and our souls washed through his most precious
> blood . . .**

This restores the ending of the prayer to its 1662 form.

The whole people of God: a note on ministries

Throughout the Church of England there are as many different ways of holding the service of Holy Communion as there are churches, and the question of who does what is an important one. This is the case not only because it helps newcomers and visiting leaders of worship to feel at home but also because our worship must both reflect and form the way in which we are the Church.

Perhaps through a shortage of clergy, or more positively through the will of God, in recent years the Church has begun to explore and learn much in the area of collaborative ministry. The two core values of collaboration in ministry are:

- first, that all Christian people are called by their baptism to exercise some ministry within the church (the title of the Church of England report *All Are Called* expresses this truth);

31

- second, that within each local church God provides the resources for ministry. Thus every church has people who are capable of leading worship, of preaching, of administration and so on.

It is important that these core values are applied to the way in which we worship God. A service in which one person does all the talking is not a valid expression of collaboration. Cardinal Suenens, the great Roman Catholic ecumenist, is said to have described this partnership in this way:

> A true leader will find his place when he has succeeded in helping others to find theirs.

While this is not exclusively a liturgical point, it does have a bearing on the way in which liturgy is planned and performed in our churches.

A new note in *Common Worship* (p. 158) gives detailed instructions on the various ministries involved in the celebration of Holy Communion. This note treads the thin but clear line between collaboration and the exercise of duly authorized ministry in liturgy. A visit to our four churches will help us to see some of the choices.

The PCC at **St Matthew's** was pleased to see the reference to the deacon in the note on ministries (p. 158) as it seemed to give official sanction to their practice of some years. The liturgical role of the deacon is shared among all those who are episcopally authorized or ordained (priest, deacon and reader) and is usually the person who is preaching.

At **St Mark's** the vicar is usually the only person with training and experience in leading worship and so he tends to lead most of the service. Lay people do read the scripture passages and lead the intercessions and encouragement is being given to those who volunteer to attend training courses.

Lay involvement at **St Luke's** is widespread. An authorized person leads the first part of a Communion service, up to the Peace. There has been heated debate in the PCC over whether or not this person should be allowed to pronounce the absolution. This has centred round the argument that the forgiveness comes from God, who has no need of mediators. Although strong views were exchanged, the PCC accepted the traditional view of the absolution being restricted in the 'you' form to ordained ministers.

St Luke's has a Lay Leadership Team which provides much of the regular ministry in the parish. This team is mandated through the Diocesan Ordained Local Ministry Scheme and its members are licensed by the Bishop to lead worship and preach and they take full advantage of the note concerning ministries (p. 158) for the first part of the service.

At **St John's**, the role of the laity is emphasized by the Liturgy of the Word, up to the Peace, being led by a churchwarden until the vicar arrives from another church in the benefice.

In what follows, Chapters 2–5 apply principally to Order One, either in contemporary or traditional language, because this is the service most commonly used. Chapter 6 comments on Order Two, again in both contemporary and traditional language.

The division of material has been made according to the four main headings in the text of Order One. This division is not in tension with the deep structure seen by the Liturgical Commission but is, rather, a simple way of dividing the text.

Main headings	Deep structure
The Gathering	Gathering
The Liturgy of the Word	Transformation
The Liturgy of the Sacrament	
The Dismissal	Mission

2 The Lord is here: Gathering for worship

It may seem self-evident to suggest that the first part of the service is the Gathering, and yet this is not simply a functional act of people coming together. Rather it is the coming together of the people of God for a particular activity, namely worship.

In Order One, *Common Worship* contains a change of emphasis from *The Alternative Service Book 1980* in the first section of the service. Here, for the first time, we see a focus on the significance of gathering together for worship. And this in itself gives the chance to ask important questions such as:

'Why are you here?'

'What has happened to you in the last few days or since you last gathered to worship?'

Each of these things is part of the luggage that worshippers bring with them and offer to the God 'from whom no secrets are hidden'.

Preparation

It is in this light that *Common Worship* provides us with an opportunity to encourage a deeper sense of preparation. When asked how long he prayed each day, Archbishop Michael Ramsey is reputed to have said that he prayed for two minutes. His questioner was surprised at the brevity of the Archbishop's prayer and so asked for an explanation. The Archbishop replied:

'I spend 28 minutes getting ready and 2 minutes praying!'

Gathering for worship and preparing ourselves should not be

ignored as we speed on towards what some might see as the real meat of the service in word and sacrament:

> The preparation is of far greater importance and involves far greater diversity of practice than many of us realise. (Kenneth Stevenson)

The notes in the ASB encouraged 'careful devotional preparation' but *Common Worship* goes one step further by providing a variety of texts entitled 'A Form of Preparation'.

The texts provided in this section are all familiar, but in some ways many of them have been marginalized in current usage. Their inclusion as a sort of preface to the main texts offers the chance to reinstate these old favourites. It also reflects a desire on the part of the Liturgical Commission to reaffirm the importance of a 'knapsack' of texts to which people may refer throughout their lives.

The texts are:

Veni Creator Spiritus

Exhortation (below)

As we gather at the Lord's table we must recall the promises and warnings given to us in the Scriptures and so examine ourselves and repent of our sins.
We should give thanks to God for his redemption of the world through his Son Jesus Christ and, as we remember Christ's death for us and receive the pledge of his love, resolve to serve him in holiness and righteousness all the days of our life.

The Commandments
Summary of the Law   } One of these
The Comfortable Words   } on any one occasion
The Beatitudes
Confession: 'Father eternal, giver of light and grace . . .'
Absolution

The notes here suggest three ways of using this material:

- By individuals as part of their private preparation. This might be at home before leaving for church (there are parallels to this in the funeral services which provide prayer for use at home before the funeral), or by printing appropriate prayers in seasonal service booklets for use in the quiet moments before worship.

- Corporately, replacing the 'Prayer of Preparation' and 'Prayers of Penitence'.

- As a separate service, perhaps a Vigil on Saturday evening, in which case a greeting is added at the start and the Peace and the Lord's Prayer at the end. It is unlikely that people will gather simply for this act of preparation. However, it might be part of a gathering of those who are to lead worship or who prepare the church for Sunday; alternatively, it might form the conclusion of another activity on a Saturday evening.

Gathering

The simplest form of Gathering introduces the Trinitarian ascription, 'In the name of the Father, and of the Son, and of the Holy Spirit' and a simple 'The Lord be with you'. But also in the main text for the first time are longer greetings, first seen in *Lent, Holy Week, Easter* (CHP/SPCK, 1984, 1986):

Grace, mercy and peace
from God our Father
and the Lord Jesus Christ
be with you

Whichever text is selected, perhaps on a seasonal basis, it should be remembered that (for those who remember the Two Ronnies) this is the 'Hello, good evening and welcome' of worship. These opening words are significant; they begin the relationship between president and congregation and should normally not be delegated to an assistant minister. The exception to this rule is when, in the absence of the priest who will preside at the Liturgy of the Sacrament, the Liturgy of the Word is presided over by an authorized lay person.

Michael Perham writes of the significance of this point in the service like this:

> It is in this exchange that individuals are brought into relationship with the president and, through him, with each other. Men, women and children become the congregation. (*Lively Sacrifice*, SPCK, 1997, p. 95)

For this greeting to follow a more informal 'Good Morning' really defeats the point of a liturgical greeting. The other way round makes more sense.

Common Worship also makes a distinction between Greeting and Acclamations. For example:

This is the day that the Lord has made.
All **Let us rejoice and be glad in it.**

Or

Alleluia. Christ is risen.
All **He is risen indeed. Alleluia.**

These are not greetings, they are acclamations (from *Patterns for Worship* and Order One) and should be used in addition to the Greeting.

The Prayer of Preparation (Collect for Purity) is optional and, if familiarity is not to lead to contempt, it might be used sparingly. However, it should be noted that it does form a part of the 'knapsack' and is a favourite prayer with many congregations. The following points should be considered when thinking about its use:

- if preceded by a hymn, its gathering nature is less obvious;

- if the Prayers of Penitence are at the early point in the service it might seem to duplicate the penitential material;

- an occasional use on Sundays and a regular use at other times might be most appropriate;

- it is a calling down of the Holy Spirit at the beginning of the service.

Whatever choices are made, at this point and at all others, the thinking behind it should be explained to the congregation. For some suggestions about how this might be done see Chapter 10.

The Prayers of Penitence

Good reasons can be given for the Prayers of Penitence to be at the start of the service or at a later point in response to the Liturgy of the Word. The notes in *Common Worship*, however, give greater freedom in placing the confession than in the ASB.

> This section may be transposed to a later point in the service as a response to the Liturgy of the Word. (Note 10, p. 331)

Position	Rationale	Texts
Before opening hymn	On special occasions, for for example the First Sunday of Advent or Ash Wednesday	From A Form of Preparation Or a Kyrie confession
As part of the Gathering	The normal position: confession is a necessary precursor of worship	Optional Summary of the Law, Law, 'God so loved the world . . .' and choice of confession. Any authorized text may also be used (Note 10).
In Liturgy of the Word	To focus on a reading with a penitential context, the confession might come after the New Testament reading*	Any authorized text
Following the Sermon	In response to issues raised in the sermon	Any authorized text
Before the Peace	Making reference to Matthew 5.23-24	Texts from Gathering

*For example, Proper 10 of Year A has Romans 8.1-11, 'For the law of the Spirit of life in Christ Jesus has set you free from the law of sin and of death', and Matthew 13.1-9, the Parable of the Sower. These readings might suggest confession in the light of the Romans passage, leading into a new openness to hear the Parable of the Sower.

The introduction to the confession

The introduction to the Prayer of Penitence is another area in which variety can be introduced. This may be seasonal, by using the texts provided in the Seasonal Provisions. For example:

From Ash Wednesday until the Saturday after the Fourth Sunday of Lent

The sacrifice of God is a broken spirit;
a broken and contrite heart God will not despise.
Let us come to the Lord, who is full of compassion,
and acknowledge our transgressions in penitence and faith.

cf Psalm 51.17

Trinity Sunday

God the Father forgives us in Christ and heals us by the Holy
    Spirit.
Let us therefore put away all anger and bitterness,
    all slander and malice,
and confess our sins to God our redeemer.

cf Ephesians 4.30, 32

Alternatively, the introduction to confession may link with the Bible readings for the day. Using the example from Proper 10 of Year A:

> There is therefore now no condemnation for those who are in Christ Jesus. For the law of the Spirit of life in Christ Jesus has set you free from the law of sin and of death. Let us confess our sins that we may set our minds on the things of the Spirit.

More formally, this might be an opportunity to use some of the texts in the Form of Preparation.

Kyrie confessions

Provision is also made for the use of the Kyrie Eleison as a confession, although not normally on Sundays (note 10, p. 331).

This will be a new idea to many people, but its use, especially at weekday services, brings a new dimension to the penitential material. Short penitential sentences, relating to the theme of the readings or the season, are inserted between the petitions of the Kyrie Eleison. A selection of these is given in the Supplementary Texts in *Common Worship*; the following example (p. 277) is based on Psalm 51:

> Wash me thoroughly from my wickedness
> and cleanse me from my sin.
> Lord, have mercy.
> *All* **Lord, have mercy.**
>
> Make me a clean heart, O God,
> and renew a right spirit within me.
> Christ, have mercy.
> *All* **Christ, have mercy.**
>
> Cast me not away from your presence,
> and take not your holy spirit from me.
> Lord, have mercy.
> *All* **Lord, have mercy.**

Other examples of Kyrie confessions may be found in *Enriching the Christian Year* (SPCK/Alcuin Club, 1993) and *Patterns for Worship* (CHP, 1995).

Gloria in Excelsis

The Gloria is a song of praise. This is perhaps most obviously seen in its position after the Communion service in *The Book of Common Prayer* (and in Order Two of *Common Worship*). However, other texts might be used according to the style of the celebration, the season of the year or the theme of the service. For example:

- At a Communion service at which children are present, a responsive Gloria such as the 'Peruvian Gloria' from *Hymns Old and New* (published by Kevin Mayhew), or the 'Lourdes Gloria'.

- Some modern songs lend themselves to use at this point of the service. 'From the rising of the Sun' or 'I will enter his gates with thanksgiving in my heart' are examples of this.

As a song of praise, the Gloria is best sung and there are a large number of settings for this and other parts of the service (see Chapter 8 on music).

The traditional omission of the Gloria during Advent and Lent, and on weekdays which are not principal holy days or festivals, is mentioned in note 11 (p. 331).

The Collect

The Collect is a presidential prayer, said on behalf of the congregation. It concludes the Gathering by collect-ing our prayers. Michael Perham describes this as being 'drawn deeper into our relationship with God and one another' before the liturgy can proceed.

The Collects in *Calendar, Lectionary and Collects* do not relate to the readings for a particular day; instead, they are fixed to Sunday names. This is explained in the notes to *Calendar, Lectionary and Collects*:

> Thus, for instance, the Collect for the Second Sunday after Trinity will always be the same, though the readings will change, depending not only on the stage of the three year cycle, but also the date on which the Second Sunday after Trinity falls in any particular year. (p. 250)

The note in the text of *Common Worship* encourages a period of silent preparation before the Collect. The silence is introduced with the words 'Let us pray' (as mentioned specifically in the note) or 'a more specific bidding'.

This opportunity for silence should not be missed, but it does need to be focused. Simply leaving a pause will make the congregation think that the president has forgotten what comes next!

Using the same Collect for the Second Sunday after Trinity ('Lord, you have taught us that all our doings without love are nothing worth . . .'), an example of the added focus might be:

> Let us pray for grace that we might reveal your love in our lives . . .
>
> *Silence*
>
> Collect

Or, for Advent Sunday

> As we wait in eager longing for the coming of God's Kingdom, let us pray that wc may live in the light of Christ . . .
>
> *Silence*
>
> Collect

However, care should be taken not to set up two conflicting themes, that of the Collect or of the readings, as you enter into the Liturgy of the Word.

Our four churches each approach the Gathering in their own way.

At **St Matthew's** some of the seasonal booklets have a different preparatory prayer printed on the inside cover. The Summary of the Law for Lent and the *Veni Creator Spiritus* for the book used at Pentecost provide a varied form of preparation.

A procession marks the start of the service: servers, the choir and clergy pass through the congregation from the back of the church. A well-bound Book of the Gospels is carried aloft and placed open on the altar by the deacon. St Matthew's welcomes the Trinitarian ascription since it confirms their practice of some years.

The Gloria is sung to one of the three settings that they use regularly and the melody line is printed in the service booklet. The president introduces the Collect with a sentence linked to the prayer that is to follow and then a short silence.

The vestry at **St Mark's** is alongside the chancel, making formal entry for the vicar difficult; he also hopes to be informal and welcoming. In the past, he has greeted the people, given out the notices for the week and then announced the hymn. After the hymn he then used the liturgical greeting, 'The Lord be with you'. However, from his reading of the notes in *Common Worship* he sees that this is not best practice and now tries to be informal within the spirit of the notes and the texts. He therefore uses the following order:

- Hymn

- Greeting

- Prayer of Preparation

- Informal welcome, leading into an introduction to confession (he has moved the notices to immediately before the Prayers of Intercession)

- Confession.

He recognizes that the choice of hymn at this point is important as it sets the mood for the rest of the service.

The 'Peruvian Gloria' is a favourite with the congregation; each line of music is sung first by a cantor and then the congregation repeats the same line. It has three verses addressed to Father, Son and Holy Spirit respectively.

The Collect is printed on a weekly pew leaflet and said by all the congregation together. The Collect is introduced with the usual 'Let us pray', which is followed by a short silence and then the vicar says, 'Let us gather our prayers together in the words of the Collect'.

Pre-service praise is a regular feature of worship at **St Luke's**, with ten minutes or so of songs leading into the service. The transition from this to the service itself is generally a few moments of silence followed by the greeting. They take advantage of the freedom to use other acclamations, which link with the Bible readings for the day.

The worship planning group has agreed that they will decide where the Prayers of Penitence are placed in the service in the light of the Bible readings. When they decide that confession should be a response to the word they include the Prayer of Preparation; when penitence comes in the early position, they omit it.

The Gloria is seldom sung at St Luke's. Instead a version of a psalm or another song of praise is used.

The texts for all the material used in the service are shown on an overhead projector screen, making it easy on occasions for the Collect to be said by the whole congregation.

At **St John's** the small choir processes into the choir stalls followed by the lay person leading the Liturgy of the Word. In the absence of the person who is to preside at the Liturgy of the Sacrament, who is at another church in the benefice, this person presides until the Peace. It is hoped that by then the priest will have arrived!

Limited resources mean that they have printed one book for their Family Service and one for other services. The Family Service begins like this:

> *As the Choir enters we sing a hymn*
> The Lord be with you
> *All* **and also with you.**
>
> This is the day that the Lord has made
> *All* **Let us rejoice and be glad in it.**
>
> **WE CONFESS**
>
> *All* **Most merciful God,**
> **Father of our Lord Jesus Christ,**
> **we confess that we have sinned**
> **in thought, word and deed.**
> **We have not loved you with our whole heart.**
> **We have not loved our neighbours as ourselves.**
> **In your mercy**
> **forgive what we have been,**

help us to amend what we are,
and direct what we shall be;
that we may do justly,
love mercy,
and walk humbly with you, our God.
Amen.

Or after each section of sentences, this response is used:

Lord, have mercy.
All **Lord, have mercy.**
Christ, have mercy.
All **Christ, have mercy.**
Lord, have mercy.
All **Lord, have mercy.**

ABSOLUTION

A SONG OF PRAISE

THE COLLECT   *a special prayer for today*

WE LISTEN TO THE WORD OF GOD

This forms a common opening to the service whether or
not it is Holy Communion. This form allows for a song of
praise such as 'I will enter his gates with thanksgiving in
my heart' or 'God is good!' to take the place of the
Gloria.

3 Hear the Gospel of our Lord Jesus Christ

Having gathered together as the people of God, we are now ready to hear his word for us. It has been said 'We are a people of the Word' and, in partnership with the sacraments, it is here that we find food for the journey. In some places a greater emphasis will be placed on the word while in others more attention will be given to the sacrament and this will reflect the underlying theology of the community. But one should never be allowed to overshadow the other. A cursory Liturgy of the Word with a five-minute homily will not feed the people of God; but equally, if the ministry of the sacrament is simply tacked on to the 'important bit' then the balance is tipped the other way.

It will be noted that this section is called the Liturgy of the Word, not the Ministry of the Word. This follows the example set in *Common Worship: Initiation Services*. It comes about through a recognition that the use of the word 'ministry' has changed. It is now used to denote a particular function exercised by an individual, such as a ministry of intercession or encouragement.

Once again, within the basic building blocks of *Common Worship* there is much variety that can be used to ensure that the word really is heard and that its relationship to the sacrament is held in proper balance.

The lectionary

Calendar, Lectionary and Collects (CLC) is the lectionary provision in *Common Worship*. The lectionary is based on the Revised Common Lectionary, an ecumenical lectionary used widely throughout the world. In the CLC version it provides a three-year cycle of readings for the Principal Service and Second and Third Services, collects for each Sunday of the year and readings and collects for saints' days and special occasions.

The Principal Service lectionary offers a semi-continuous reading of the Synoptic Gospels in three years, with St John used in festal seasons. In Ordinary Time there is a choice between a semi-continuous reading of both an Old Testament and New Testament book, or an Old Testament reading that is related to the Gospel with the semi-continuous New Testament readings. The table below shows the different options in Propers 4–6 of Year A.

	Proper 4	Proper 5	Proper 6
Old Testament *Continuous:*	Genesis 6: Noah	Genesis 12: Call of Abram	Genesis 18: Abraham and the three men
Related:	Deuteronomy 11: The choice between obeying the commandments of God or following other gods	Hosea 5.15f.: Come, let us return to the Lord	Exodus 19.2f.: Listen to me and keep my covenant
New Testament	Romans 1.16f.: The righteous will live by faith	Romans 4.13f.: Not by law but by righteousness	Romans 5 Justified by faith
Gospel	Matthew 7.21f.: The houses built on rock and sand	Matthew 9.9f.: Call of Matthew	Matthew 9.35f.: The crop is heavy but the labourers are few

So, once again, there are choices to be made:

- Which is our Principal Service?

- In Ordinary Time, are we going to follow the related stream of readings or the semi-continuous one?

- Do we celebrate saints' days? During the week and on Sundays?

These choices are best made at the start of the new year, before Advent. In this way a detailed programme of Bible reading and preaching can be established for the coming year, ensuring that a balance is maintained between the Old and New Testaments. The main benefit, however, is that Scripture is not reduced to bite-sized chunks, but is offered to congregations in context.

CLC also offers an open season for readings (p. 249; note 7 in *Common Worship*, p. 540). Between the Feast of the Presentation of Christ and Ash Wednesday and again between Trinity Sunday and the First Sunday of Advent, the notes in *Calendar, Lectionary and Collects* allow local lectionary provision. This provides the flexibility to look at a particular theme of readings, perhaps at a suitable time of year.

- A creation-centred theme might be appropriate in October. See, for example, *The Season of Creation* (Episcopal Environmental Coalition, 200 Main Street, Chatham, New Jersey 07928). This provides a variety of scriptural and non-scriptural readings, hymns and songs and liturgical texts.

- A more thematic approach to the reading of Old Testament history might be adopted, thus overcoming the predominantly primary-school view of the Old Testament possessed by many congregations!

However, it should be pointed out that the provision made in *Calendar, Lectionary and Collects* is the '*normative* lectionary provision' (CLC, p. 248; CW, p. 540).

Beware of semi-continuous Christians!

There is a danger inherent in this lectionary which is related to current patterns of churchgoing. Many churches are aware that regular members of the congregation do not attend every Sunday, as has been confirmed by the recent publication of church attendance figures. Instead, a pattern of regular churchgoing every two or three weeks is emerging. So we have to be careful in preaching that we do not assume that the whole congregation has been on the same journey through the Letter to the Ephesians, for example. This is also a danger in multi-church benefices, where it is important to make the right choice about which is the Principal Service on each Sunday in each church.

For more detail on *Calendar, Lectionary and Collects*, the changes that it makes to our way of reading the Bible and how to introduce it, see Mark Earey's useful *Praxis* Lectionary Training Pack. For a more detailed examination of the provision and the background to it, see Michael Perham's book *Celebrate the Christian Story* (SPCK, 1997).

Honouring the saints

Calendar, Lectionary and Collects provides four principles on which the observance of Holy Days is based:

- the Church is enriched by the celebration of its fellowship with the saints;
- that celebration should not detract from the cycle of the seasons nor of Sundays;
- a simple categorization of observance is helpful;
- the Church of England does not canonize.

CLC provides a more extensive calendar of saints than the ASB or BCP. The categories are under three headings:

- Festivals;
- Lesser Festivals;
- Commemorations.

Detailed rules for the transferring of saints' days from Sundays can be found in CLC.

Useful material for the saints, including readings, a Collect and post communion prayer and a short biography can be found in *Exciting Holiness* (Brother Tristam SSF, Canterbury Press, 1997).

Reading the word

There is little point in reading if the reader can neither be seen nor heard. This very basic point offers us the possibility of doing more than simply reading the given passage from a lectern placed at a good vantage point in the church, although this will be the norm.

In order to avoid inaudibility, training might be offered to all those who read in church. A short course could be organized both for those who have been reading for years and for newcomers. The course might include advice on:

- how to introduce a passage, giving chapter and verse;

- how to explain the background to the passage;

- contextualizing the passage: for example, saying who the speaker is. 'Jesus said: The Kingdom of Heaven . . .' is much easier to understand than 'The Kingdom of heaven . . .';

- pronouncing proper names;

- the use of a PA system, if there is one.

Equally, if the same presentation of the word of God is used week after week, the immediacy of Scripture may be lost. *The Dramatised Bible* (Marshall Pickering/Bible Society, 1989) provides simple versions of most Bible passages for two or more voices. It should not be thought that this can only be used in Family or Parade Services, since a different way of hearing the word can communicate well to all ages and in many situations.

Variety can also be achieved in other ways. The Bible Society and the BBC have produced audio tapes of the Bible read by leading actors. On Bible Sunday, for example, one of the tapes might be played instead of reading the Gospel.

Psalmody

The notes indicate that three readings are usually to be read and that the psalm or canticle should be used following the Old Testament reading to which it relates. Since the decline of Matins and Evensong in many churches, the Psalms have become a marginal part of Scripture for some. Here we have a chance to restore the Psalms and enable our congregations to learn from the all-encompassing view of human experience and our relationship with God contained within them.

There are many different ways in which the psalms can be used:

- Using books such as *Psalms and Music for the Eucharist*, a collection of responsorial psalms in which a cantor sings the verses and the congregation joins in a simple response, or *Psalm Songs*, a collection of songs based on the Psalms (see resources section, p. 112).

- Reading the psalms antiphonally: a leader reads one verse and the congregation the next.

- Anglican chant: this is really not as inaccessible as many people think, provided that the congregation is given pointed versions of the text and some explanation of how the system works.

- Plainsong might also be considered.

Gospel Acclamations

Common Worship provides short, biblical acclamations for use immediately before the reading of the Gospel. These are biblical texts, surrounded by 'alleluias', which serve to emphasize the primary place of the good news in our worship. Seven of these are provided for Ordinary Time, on page 280, and seasonal texts are contained within the seasonal provision of the Supplementary Texts.

These Gospel Acclamations have been set to very simple chants, which can further emphasize the reading of the Gospel.

During Lent the 'Alleluia' is replaced with:

Praise to you, O Christ, King of eternal glory.

Preaching the word

In a society in which the scenes on *Eastenders* never last more than 45 seconds, the expectation we have of congregations to listen carefully to a 20-minute monologue might seem optimistic.

Yet there is a place for solid expository preaching as a part of a wider range of techniques for expounding the word of God. *Common Worship* continues the development made first in *A Service of the Word*, which gives sanction to the wide range of styles and techniques used by those who preach the word (Note 7, p. 27).

> The term 'sermon' includes less formal exposition, the use of drama, interviews, discussion, audio-visuals and the insertion of hymns or other sections of the service between parts of the sermon.

At **St Matthew's** the focus for the Liturgy of the Word is a large lectern in a similar style to the altar. Here the word is read and sermons are preached, showing clearly that the church believes that word and sacrament have equal standing in their worship.

The three readings from *Calendar, Lectionary and Collects* are used and great care is given to choosing which stream is to be followed. This is done at biannual meetings held just before Advent and in Eastertide, attended by all those who will preach regularly in the coming six months.

The choir leads responsorial psalms. These have been well received as a simple way into the use of psalms in worship. The Gospel Book, placed on the altar at the start of the service, is carried by the reader, usually the deacon, to the lectern accompanied by acolytes; on festivals incense is used. As part of the introduction to the Gospel, the choir sings the Gospel Acclamations, with congregational responses.

Saints' days are observed according to the notes in *Calendar, Lectionary and Collects*. The main emphasis on Sundays is a celebration of the Resurrection, so only Festivals which fall on Sundays are observed; Festivals which fall on weekdays are not transferred to Sunday. Instead, those Festivals and Lesser Festivals are observed by making use of *Exciting Holiness* (see resources section, p. 112).

The preaching team meets each month to discuss with each other how they will approach particular lectionary readings. Their discussions are based on a book by Bishop Paul Marshall, *Preaching for the Church Today* (Church Hymnal Corporation, New York, 1990).

The PCC at **St Mark's** has decided that three readings is too many for its very mixed congregation and so the vicar makes a choice between the Old and the New Testament readings. He has learnt the hard way that he has to prepare carefully and in advance so as to avoid beginning a semi-continuous reading at Chapter 7! They say the psalms using a congregational response and use the Gospel Acclamations.

The vicar was forcibly struck by the opening scenes of the film *Priest*. In these scenes the priest of a church in a poor area of Liverpool walks round the church in conversation with his congregation. Those who preach at St Mark's have adopted this dialogue style, believing that this enables the congregation to participate and to think for themselves.

Saints' days are observed only if they fall on a day when there would otherwise be a service.

The Worship Team at **St Luke's** welcomes the structure of the *Calendar, Lectionary and Collects*, since it confirms their practice of reading through entire books rather than filleted excerpts. They also welcome the 'open seasons' during which they have created their own series of readings.

On occasion a song between the readings will be based on the psalm set for the day, but generally the choice of music is more on the theme that the preacher has selected from one of the readings.

St Luke's takes full advantage of note 7 and uses a variety of dramatic presentations, dance and more formal preaching styles. However, they also ensure that these different ways of opening Scripture up to the congregation are used carefully and in a balanced way. Their emphasis is on exposition.

Saints' days are not usually observed at St Luke's.

A lay person conducts the Liturgy of the Word at **St John's**, and this is usually the same person who preaches that day. At the Family Service, where the parish has seen most growth in recent years, only two readings are used. They try always to have a good story as one of the readings to enable the children to participate in the reading and its explanation.

On other occasions three readings are used and the psalm is read.

Responding to God's word

The reading of God's word and its exposition, by whatever means seem appropriate, will lead to a desire to respond to that word, both in affirmation and in intercession. However, both of these responses can become habit rather than a real response to God and his promises to us in Scripture. *Common Worship* provides alternative forms of creeds and intercession, to enable the people of God to make their corporate and individual response to God.

Silence as a response to God's word

The temptation to keep the service moving is often great. This might be because of a time constraint or simply to keep up the momentum of the drama. However, we should not forget that a period of silent reflection after hearing God's word or after the sermon can allow themes to develop within the mind of the worshipper.

In order to encourage the congregation to use this time creatively, the reader or preacher might remain in place for the period of silence, only moving back to their seat at the end.

I believe

A Service of the Word provides 13 alternative forms of Creed and
Affirmation of Faith and in *Common Worship* there is a version
of the Nicene Creed without the *filioque*, 'suitable for use on
ecumenical occasions'. One of the alternatives may be sung to
one of several well-known hymn tunes, others emphasize
particular themes or biblical passages.

Let us pray to the Father

The second response of the people to the word of God is to offer
him praise and thanksgiving for his love in 'our creation,
preservation and all the blessings of this life' (as *The Book of
Common Prayer* puts it), and to seek his blessing on those concerns
and people held in common by the gathered congregation.

However, a question that arises in my mind as I participate in the
'Prayers of the People' is 'To whom are these prayers addressed?'
Are they truly offered to God or, as is sometimes the case, are
they a commentary on the life of the congregation offered by one
of its members? The notes concerning the intercessions explain
this clearly (p. 281):

> *This form may be used either with the insertion of specific
> subjects between the paragraphs or as a continuous whole, with
> or without brief biddings addressed to the people before the
> prayer begins.*

So while the biddings are addressed to the people, prayer itself is
addressed to God.

The main text of *Common Worship* includes two alternative
versicles and responses for use in the prayers.

> Lord, in your mercy
> *All* **hear our prayer.**
>
> *(or)*
>
> Lord, hear us.
> *All* **Lord, graciously hear us.**

However, the notes also allow for a variety of versicles and responses to the intercession. A selection of these may be found in *Patterns for Worship* and *Enriching the Christian Year* and could be used in seasonal service books. It is important, even if these responses are printed, that the leader tells the congregation which response is being used.

Some examples from the Christian year are:

Advent

The response to the petition 'Maranatha' is '**Come, Lord Jesus**'. *(Patterns for Worship*, p. 66)

Epiphany

The response to the petition 'Light of the world' is '**Shine in our darkness**'. (Susan Sayers, *Living Stones Year C*)

Lent

The response to the petition 'Lord of compassion' is '**in your mercy hear us**'. (*Enriching the Christian Year*, p. 1)

These responses might be used for an entire season; however, there are many collections of prayers containing examples for each Sunday of the year with a different versicle and response (see, for example, *Enriching the Christian Year*, *More Prayers for Sunday* (HarperCollins, 1997), *Prayers of Intercession* (Kevin Mayhew, 2000) and the *Living Stones* series).

Music can also provide a suitable response to the sections of the prayer. A good example of this is the Taizé chant, 'O Lord, hear my prayer'. The organ accompaniment to this simple tune can be varied in each repetition of it and the more adventurous might like to use the *ostinato* parts written for different instruments and published by Taizé Press (for other resources see Chapters 8 and 11).

All these points should be clearly made in any training that is offered to those who lead the prayers of the people, so that by prayerful preparation they can lead the people in their prayers.

In each of our churches lay people normally lead the Prayers of Intercession. However, the style used varies from place to place.

St Matthew's prints a seasonal response in its service booklets and encourages the leaders to use them, unless there is to be a musical response. The leaders have all been on a three-session course. The sessions were entitled:

- Personal prayer life as a springboard to public prayer;

- 'Lesbian whales against the Bomb!' Don't try to do too much;

- An evening at the Diocesan Resource Room.

An emphasis is placed on periods of silence between the sections of the prayers.

At **St Mark's** the vicar has told the people who lead the prayers that the five headings, Church, creation, community, the sick and the departed, are the best way to focus the prayers of the people. However, he believes that the world should come before the Church and so encourages people to swap them round. He also sees the parish notices as a good source for the prayers of the congregation and so reads them before the Prayers of Intercession.

The Prayers of Intercession are another place in which the emphasis on the gifts of the Spirit is seen at **St Luke's**. This is true both in the words used and in the style of preparation that is encouraged before leading the prayers. References to the Spirit are frequent and those who lead are likely to have spent more time in private prayer than with a pen and paper making notes. The OHP is sometimes used to display pictures or headings for prayer. Occasionally time is given for open prayer in which members of the congregation are encouraged to participate.

The leaders of prayer at **St John's** have found the wide variety of resources available most helpful in preparing their own prayers. In particular they have used material written by Susan Sayers (see resources section, p. 115). As they have grown in confidence they are now more likely to use her work as a basis for writing their own prayers.

4 Remembering Jesus

Having prepared ourselves for worship, confessed our sins and heard the word of God, we now move into the third of the four sections of Holy Communion identified earlier.

The Peace

In a choir vestry of my acquaintance hangs a cartoon proclaiming that the church is a 'Peace-free zone'! Of course, what the cartoonist objects to is not the principle of reconciliation with our neighbour before approaching the holy table, as derived from the teaching of Jesus in Matthew 5, but rather its outworking in the simple instruction

> *All may exchange a sign of peace.*

The Peace, although widely accepted, remains a bone of contention in some places and may need to be handled sensitively. It does, however, have the capacity to break down the inhibitions of worshippers and enable people to enter more fully into the relationship between God and his people. This relationship has two dimensions, the vertical and the horizontal, and at its best is a dynamic one with space for growth in both dimensions.

The provision in *Common Worship* is similar to that in the ASB, except that neither of the two familiar sentences of introduction are in the main text. Instead they are included in the seven texts provided in the Supplementary Texts (p. 290). There are also texts for introducing the Peace in each section of the Seasonal Provisions.

The ASB allowed the Peace to be used in a different place as occasion demands. This permission is made clearer in *Common Worship* by note 16 (p. 333).

> The peace follows naturally from the prayers of intercession and begins the Liturgy of the Sacrament. But this section may be transposed to be the opening greeting or may be used later in the service, as part of either the breaking of bread or the Dismissal.

This freedom dramatically alters the point of this section in the service. As an opening greeting, the Peace changes the emphasis from Gathering into that of an introduction agency, to ensure that everybody knows the person sitting next to them. Placing the Peace at the breaking of the bread, as in the Roman Catholic rite, on the other hand, provides a liturgical link between 'Forgive us our sins as we forgive those who sin against us' and the final phrase of the Agnus Dei, 'Grant us peace'. Finally, the Peace may be used as part of the Dismissal, linking the blessing, 'The peace of God . . .' with 'Go in peace to love and serve the Lord'.

However, it is probably right that the default setting remains the familiar position with its biblical echo in the teaching of Jesus. The Peace, if used here and 'exchanged', leads appropriately into the hymn which may be sung during the Preparation of the Table.

At **St Matthew's,** full use is made of the seasonal texts available to introduce the Peace and the deacon invites the congregation to exchange peace, saying, 'Let us offer a sign of God's peace to our neighbour'. The hymn at the Preparation of the Table is not announced (the number is shown on the hymn board). The organist simply begins to play when he thinks that people have had long enough to carry out this instruction!

The Peace at **St Mark's** sometimes seems more like a half-time break! Members of the congregation take the opportunity to catch up with their friends and this is encouraged by the vicar, who sees the importance of the fellowship of the church for the many lonely people who attend St Mark's.

There are occasions when half-time break is exactly what the Peace is at **St Luke's,** since the PCC decided to serve refreshments at this point at services with a focus on newcomers. The rationale is that they want to encourage new people but recognize that the Liturgy of the Sacrament is not always accessible to them.

So people visiting the church for the first time are encouraged to attend the Liturgy of the Word, which is followed by coffee. After this short break there follows a choice of activity. Some will attend the Liturgy of the Sacrament, while newcomers are offered the opportunity to join a discussion group. As a result of this, the parish notices are given out before the Peace.

At **St John's** the Peace forms an appropriate moment for the priest, who has been at another church in the benefice already that morning, to greet the congregation and take over leadership for the Liturgy of the Sacrament.

However, the Peace is not universally accepted and is therefore only exchanged at the Family Eucharist.

Taking of the Bread and Wine

Note 36 of the ASB (p. 130) is one of those rubrics that covers a multitude of practice, there being enormous variety in the way in which different churches get the bread, wine and possibly the money from one place to another.

Common Worship simplifies this a little. Note 17 (p. 333) tells us that the president must take the bread and the wine into his or her hands either after the table is prepared or during the eucharistic prayer. There still remains much scope for liturgical action at this point.

Kenneth Stevenson calls this one of the 'soft points' of Holy Communion and asks the question:

in what sense is the preparation of the gifts a functional act, in what sense symbolic. (*Liturgy for a New Century*, SPCK/Alcuin Club, 1991)

At its most simple this will involve bringing the bread and the wine from a side table of some description; the most complex will include processions and incense. Whatever action is used, the basic principles should not be lost:

- Here the church follows the example of Jesus in taking the bread and the wine, giving thanks over them, breaking the bread and giving the elements to the gathered congregation. These four actions, identified by Dom Gregory Dix in *The Shape of the Liturgy* (A&C Black, 1997), form the backbone of the Liturgy of the Sacrament.

- The first of these actions, taking, gives the opportunity to reflect on the overflowing goodness of God in his creation.

- Do we offer the gifts or bring them?

This last point requires some exploration. One way into the subject is to look at the 'Table Prayers' given sanction by note 33 in the ASB.

> The president may praise God for his gifts in appropriate words to which all respond
> **Blessed be God for ever.**

It is envisaged that the praise to God will be in the form of a Jewish Table Blessing as in the Roman Catholic offertory prayers. These prayers emphasize that God's people offer the gifts to him. However, many will be unhappy with this language, arguing that the Eucharist is properly concerned with remembering rather than offering.

The theological position taken on this will affect the choice of Table Prayers to be used. Some will continue to use the Roman Catholic text, others will seek a compromise, retaining some 'offering' language but in respect of 'offering our sacrifice of praise'. A third option is to avoid any offering language, focusing instead on 'bringing', or on God's goodness in feeding his people. The wide variety of alternatives in the Supplementary Texts will meet a range of theological understandings of this action. It has been the aim of the compilers to provide texts that can be used by everyone, though people might choose not to use all the texts.

Several of the Table Prayers are in the form 'Blessed be God . . .' or 'Blessed are you, Lord God . . .', which lead on to the response 'Blessed be God for ever'.

Of your own do we give you

The second area of confusion surrounding this action is what to do with the money! Some churches, finding it a distraction, adopt the principle that no collection will be taken during worship and thus avoid the issue. However, if a collection is taken it is probably appropriate that it is the subject of liturgical action rather than simply placed on a table in the corner until somebody comes to count it. That is too utilitarian an approach to money and does not take advantage of the opportunity to give thanks to God for his great goodness to us in the whole of creation.

The familiar 'Yours, Lord . . .' is also in the Supplementary Texts, with the final two lines indicated as a congregational text.

> Yours, Lord, is the greatness, the power,
> the glory, the splendour, and the majesty;
> for everything in heaven and on earth is yours.
> *All* **All things come from you,**
> **and of your own do we give you.**

This prayer has a universal appeal in that it can be seen as linking the presentation of the collection with the rest of the Preparation of the Table, or as referring only to the monetary offering.

Common Worship also provides two additional prayers (see below and overleaf) that refer specifically to the presentation of the collection (2 and 3 in 'Prayers at the Preparation of the Table', p. 291).

> Generous God,
> creator, redeemer, sustainer,
> at your table we present this money,
> symbol of the work you have given us to do;
> use it, use us,
> in the service of your world
> to the glory of your name.
> *All* **Amen.**

> God of life, Saviour of the poor,
> receive with this money
> gratitude for your goodness,
> penitence for our pride
> and dedication to your service
> in Jesus Christ our Lord.
> *All* **Amen.**

These prayers focus entirely on the collection and therefore omit reference to the bread and the wine. The remaining six texts are more general in their reference.

So a choice needs to be made as to which of the variety of theological positions, and therefore texts, are to be adopted.

The Preparation of the Table at **St Matthew's** involves a procession of servers with candles, those with the bread and the wine and the stewards with the collection. The table is prepared by the deacon who turns to the president and bows when the job is done. The president then says the Table Prayers using one of the variety of texts provided in the Supplementary Texts.

On Principal Feasts and Festivals incense is used at the Preparation of the Table.

In the past at **St Mark's**, the bread, wine and collection have been brought from the back of the church. Then the people who have brought them place them on the table and fill the chalice with wine. The vicar always picks up the bread and the wine from the table and usually uses the prayer 'Yours, Lord . . .'. He likes the congregational response to it!

St Luke's adopts a more functional approach to the Preparation of the Table. The bread and wine are brought from a side table while the Peace is being exchanged, or during the coffee break on the Sundays when this happens in the middle of the service. They have decided not to use a Table Prayer since they think that it detracts from the focus of the Liturgy of the Sacrament in the eucharistic prayer. No collection is taken during the service; instead, a plate is available by the door as people arrive or leave.

The people of **St John's** have been familiar with the use of 'Yours, Lord, is the greatness . . .' at this point in the service. However, the leaders of worship recognize that in the minds of the congregation this refers only to the collection. So they have decided to use a wider selection of texts at this point in the service.

We give thanks

If doctrine in the Church of England is expressed through liturgy then one of the main areas in which we may discover the eucharistic theology of the church is in the eucharistic prayers. The sensitivity of this embodiment of doctrine in liturgy has been seen most clearly in the rejection of the six new eucharistic prayers presented to the General Synod in 1996.

The aim of the Liturgical Commission has been to provide 'sufficient variety and structure . . . to enable the diversity of cultural communities we serve to pray with integrity and understanding' (GS1299, *Eucharistic Prayer: Report by the Liturgical Commission*). The result has been eight prayers authorized for use.

The Eucharistic Prayers

The table overleaf gives a broad outline of the prayers in *Common Worship*, their origins and the main points to note.

	Origins	**Main points to note**
Prayer A	Based on ASB Prayers 1 and 2	The substantial credal opening may be omitted if a proper preface is used. An optional response, 'To you be glory and praise for ever', is provided. Extended prefaces may be used.
Prayer B	Revision of ASB Prayer 3	Textual changes: • 'was seen on earth' becomes 'lived on earth'. • 'His perfect sacrifice made once for the sins of all men' becomes 'for the sins of the whole world' (cf. John 3.16). • 'through him from whom all good things come' is omitted. Extended prefaces may be used.
Prayer C	Revision of ASB Prayer 4	Grammatical changes only, bringing this prayer closer to its BCP origins.
Prayer D	New	This prayer uses short sentences and narrative to bring the past alive in the present. It has been written with the presence and participation of children in mind, but may be used on other occasions as well.
Prayer E	New	Prayer E shares a simple narrative style with Prayer D. Its imagery is more vivid and concrete than that of the other prayers.

		This prayer provides another setting for the extended prefaces of the Supplementary Texts; when the short preface is used it is one of the shortest eucharistic prayers. Notice also that the memorial acclamation comes after the anamnesis rather than immediately after the institution narrative.
Prayer F	New	Influenced by the Liturgy of St Basil (fourth century), this form is common in other Anglican provinces. The 'Eastern' feel of the prayer brings a new sense of fervour and engagement. There is no opportunity for a proper preface. The acclamations may be said first by the deacon or other minister and then by the whole congregation.
Prayer G	ICEL (Roman Catholic)	This prayer is based on one of those rejected by the General Synod in 1996.
Prayer H	New, interactive prayer	In this prayer the sense of the prayer is moved forward by congregational responses as well as by the president. About one third of the prayer is said by the congregation.

Printed in outline only

Common Worship does not contain the full text of these prayers in context; instead, they are printed in full at the end of the service and the outline on pages 68–9 is provided in the main part of the book (pp. 176–7).

The Eucharistic Prayer

An authorized Eucharistic Prayer is used.

The president says

The Lord be with you   *(or)*   The Lord is here.
All **and also with you.**   **His Spirit is with us**.

Lift up your hearts.
All **We lift them to the Lord.**

Let us give thanks to the Lord our God.
All **It is right to give thanks and praise.**

The president praises God for his mighty acts and all respond

All **Holy, holy, holy Lord,**
God of power and might,
heaven and earth are full of your glory.
Hosanna in the highest.
[Blessed is he who comes in the name of the Lord.
Hosanna in the highest.]

The president recalls the Last Supper,
and one of these four acclamations may be used

[Great is the mystery of faith:]   [Praise to you, Lord Jesus:]
All **Christ has died:**   **Dying you destroyed**
Christ is risen: **our death,**
Christ will come again.   **rising you restored our**
                               life:
                               Lord Jesus, come in
                               glory.

[Christ is the bread of life:]   [Jesus Christ is Lord:]
All **When we eat this bread**   **Lord, by your cross**
and drink this cup,   **and resurrection**
we proclaim your death,   **you have set us free.**
Lord Jesus,   **You are the Saviour of**
until you come in glory.   **the world.**

The Prayer continues and leads into the doxology,
to which all respond boldly

All **Amen.**

Prayer A

This response may be used

All **To you be glory and praise for ever.**

and the Prayer ends

All **Blessing and honour and glory and power
be yours for ever and ever.
Amen.**

Prayer D

These words are used

This is his/our story.
All **This is our song:
Hosanna in the highest.**

and the Prayer ends

All **Blessing and honour and glory and power
be yours for ever and ever.
Amen.**

Prayer F

These responses may be used

All **Amen. Lord, we believe.**

All **Amen. Come, Lord Jesus.**

All **Amen. Come, Holy Spirit.**

Prayer G

Prayer G ends

All **Blessing and honour and glory and power
be yours for ever and ever.
Amen.**

Prayer H

For Prayer H, see page 204.

There are pros and cons with this layout. The major benefit is that the president does not need to ask the congregation to 'turn to page 184' for the Eucharistic Prayer because the common outline is printed. It also ensures that members of the congregation do not have their heads buried in the book all the time.

However, the outline is so brief that some people may get lost in trying to follow it. One way of solving this problem is the use of a seasonal booklet in which the text of only those prayers that are to be used is printed. Also, the outline does not work well with Prayer H, which has no regular response.

Extended Prefaces

Also provided is a selection of seasonal Extended Prefaces for use with Prayers A, B and E. These replace all the material before the Sanctus, but retain a sense of the familiar lead into the Sanctus. They contain echoes of familiar texts for the particular seasons.

For example, in Eastertide, with echoes of the Exultet (p. 317):

> It is indeed right, our duty and our joy . . .
> And so, in the joy of this Passover,
> earth and heaven resound with gladness,
> while angels and archangels and the powers of all creation
> sing for ever the hymn of your glory:

Or Trinity Sunday, with echoes of the Te Deum (p. 323):

> It is indeed right, our duty and our joy . . .
> We, your holy Church, acclaim you,
> Father of majesty unbounded,
> your true and only Son, worthy of all worship,
> and the Holy Spirit, advocate and guide.
> Three Persons we adore,
> one in being and equal in majesty.
> And so with angels and archangels,
> with cherubim and seraphim,
> we sing for ever of your glory:

Memorial acclamations

Several different acclamations are provided for the eucharistic prayers. Note that each has a different cue line:

> [Great is the mystery of faith:]
> **Christ has died . . .**
>
> [Christ is the bread of life:]
> **When we eat . . .**

Praying the prayers

The choice of four main prayers in the ASB led some to imagine that an appropriate way to use them would be Prayer 1 on the first Sunday of the month and so on. This is not really the best way!

Instead, the prayers might be used according to the season or with consideration given to the congregation which is likely to gather for the service. For example:

- Prayer A: Ordinary Time, the default setting.

- Prayer B, with its emphasis on salvation history, is appropriate for use at Christmastide and Eastertide.

- Prayer C, with the emphasis on the Cross, might be used in Lent and Passiontide.

- Prayer D might be suitable if children are present or on other occasions where a comparatively shorter prayer would be appropriate.

- Prayer E, with seasonal extended prefaces, could be used at the appropriate festival or season.

- Prayer F contains vivid imagery and the 'Eastern' feel of the prayer will bring new ideas into the Church's liturgical vocabulary. The prayer might be used during Advent, particularly if the optional responses are used:

> [*All* **Amen. Lord, we believe.**]
>
> [*All* **Amen. Come, Lord Jesus.**]
> [*All* **Amen. Come, Holy Spirit.**]

- Prayer G emphasizes the work of God in creation and so might be used on the Second Sunday before Lent or any other time when that theme is being used.

- Prayer H is the most radical of the prayers and some congregations may take some time to get used to it. However, it does emphasize the collaborative nature of the Body of Christ in worship.

This is only one way of using the prayers. It would be time well spent to become familiar with the texts and develop local patterns of use.

The Lord's Prayer

The Lord's Prayer, perhaps more than any other part of the service, is where the individual devotional practice of the worshippers is seen. We can all think of people who close their eyes and put their hands together as soon as the priest says 'As our Saviour has taught us'. Or again, people who have their own version, a conflation of the traditional and modern, deeply ingrained in their memories.

The desire to enable people to pray from the 'knapsack' is a good one, and it is clear that the Lord's Prayer should form a part of that supply of prayers. However, in a liturgical context we can add variety and focus to the use of well-known prayers by the way the prayer is introduced. This has the additional benefit of preventing the family prayer of Christian people from becoming habit-forming behaviour!

The following are examples of how this can be achieved.

- *In Advent*: 'Let us pray for the coming of God's kingdom in the words our Saviour taught us' (*Patterns for Worship*, p. 65).

- *At Pentecost*: 'Being made one by the power of the Spirit, let us pray as our Saviour has taught us'.

Another approach would be to focus the prayer with reference to the readings or sermon of the day. It is important, nevertheless, to ensure that familiar trigger texts are present. These include 'as our Saviour has taught us . . .' or (if traditional language is used) 'we are bold to say . . .'.

Breaking of the Bread

The third of the actions of Jesus is to break the bread. Some will wish that the instruction in *The Book of Common Prayer* ('Here the priest is to take the Paten into his hands: And here to break the Bread:') were still to be found in the middle of the Eucharistic Prayer. However, Dix's work shows that the 'Last Supper of our Lord with his disciples is the source of the liturgical Eucharist, but not the model for its performance' (*The Shape of the Liturgy*, A&C Black, 1997, p. 48).

Thus while there is no prohibition on the breaking of the bread during the Eucharistic Prayer, encouragement is given to follow the liturgical shape rather than the historical source of the actions.

Two texts for the breaking of the bread are provided, the first a familiar one from the ASB, based on 1 Corinthians 10, the second echoing 1 Corinthians 11.

We break this bread
to share in the body of Christ.

All **Though we are many, we are one body,
because we all share in one bread.**

(or)

Every time we eat this bread
and drink this cup,

All **we proclaim the Lord's death
until he comes.**

Seasonal alternatives for this point in the service may be found in *Enriching the Christian Year*.

The Breaking of the Bread at this point should include all the bread, not just a priest's wafer or a small part of the bread. The breaking is in order that the bread can be distributed.

Note 20 on the Breaking of the Bread (p. 334) indicates that the texts provided should normally be used on Sundays and principal holy days, but that the bread may be broken in silence or accompanied by the Agnus Dei at weekday celebrations.

The report of the International Anglican Liturgical Consultation (IALC) in Dublin made the point that 'no actions should make one bit of the prayer seem more significant'. A solution to this is not to dispense with all manual acts but to have more dramatic gesture throughout the prayer.

Dramatic gesture is not the only way to vary the 'performance' of the Eucharistic Prayer. The prayers contain what we might call an internal dynamic. For example, the salvation history in Prayer B contains a sense of crescendo through the paragraph.

And so, Father, calling to mind his death on the cross,
his perfect sacrifice made once for the sins of the whole
world;
rejoicing in his mighty resurrection and glorious ascension,
and looking for his coming in glory,
we celebrate this memorial of our redemption.
As we offer you this our sacrifice of praise and thanksgiving,
we bring before you this bread and this cup
and we thank you for counting us worthy
to stand in your presence and serve you.

This crescendo can be emphasized by starting the paragraph in a quiet voice which then grows not only in volume but also in intensity through the text.

We receive: the Giving of Communion

Our remembering of the actions of Jesus now reaches the fourth point, 'giving'. The default setting for the invitation to communion remains the familiar words 'Draw near with faith'. These words, with their link with the BCP, are, as Michael Perham points out, 'the classic Anglican description of what happens in receiving communion' (*Lively Sacrifice*, SPCK, 1997, p. 150).

However, *Common Worship* also offers three alternatives to these historic words in the main text.

Jesus is the Lamb of God
who takes away the sin of the world.
Blessed are those who are called to his supper.
All **Lord, I am not worthy to receive you,**
but only say the word, and I shall be healed.

(or)

God's holy gifts
for God's holy people.
All **Jesus Christ is holy,**
Jesus Christ is Lord,
to the glory of God the Father.

or, from Easter Day to Pentecost

Alleluia. Christ our passover is sacrificed for us.
All **Therefore let us keep the feast. Alleluia.**

It is important that, whichever of the four forms of invitation is used, this is an invitation to the whole congregation and comes, most appropriately, before the president and other ministers receive communion themselves. Thought might be given to the ministers of communion receiving after the rest of the congregation, as a symbol of the servant leadership of those who preside at the service and administer communion. A further way of emphasizing this is to administer communion to the ministers

75

in a circle. The president gives the paten to the person on his or her left, who then gives the president communion; the paten is passed on and the pattern repeated. The president passes the chalice to the person on his or her left in the usual way.

The Prayer of Humble Access

The final major change from the ASB is the position of the Prayer of Humble Access. In *Common Worship* it comes immediately before the distribution and thus becomes much more closely linked with the distribution and reception of communion.

Two texts are provided, both familiar from the ASB. The modern version of the traditional prayer is well known; less well known is David Frost's 'Most merciful Lord . . .'. This prayer, having been well received in the ASB, deserves its place in the main text (instead of in an appendix as in the ASB) and I would suggest that if seasonal or occasional booklets are printed, serious thought should be given to its use during certain seasons or for some services.

The distribution

Five sets of words to accompany the distribution of Holy Communion are given in the Supplementary Texts (p. 295). The inclusion of two, which have been in popular use for some years but have not appeared in authorized service books, gives them official sanction.

4
The body of Christ, broken for you.
The blood of Christ, shed for you.

5
The bread of heaven in Christ Jesus.
The cup of life in Christ Jesus.

At **St Matthew's** the use of the eucharistic prayers is in line with the suggestions made earlier. They have also been part of a trial of the new settings for singing the prayers carried out by the RSCM.

They further emphasize the seasonal aspect of their worship by varying the Acclamation. For example:

> [Jesus Christ is Lord:]
> **Lord, by your cross and**
> **resurrection . . .**

is particularly appropriate in Eastertide.

St Mark's also varies the use of the eucharistic prayers but in a rather random way. However, they are coming to like Prayer E for the variety it gives and Prayer H because of the congregational participation. They sing the Lord's Prayer using the Caribbean version (*Junior Praise*).

At **St Luke's** they tend to use Prayer D when children and young people are present and Prayer A on other occasions.

A loaf of bread is used for the Communion service, but they have realized that it is important to choose one of an appropriate size so that somebody does not have a large quantity of bread to eat afterwards.

St John's PCC decided to use the new prayers regularly for a few months before fixing a pattern of usage. They intend to use Prayer D for their Family Communion and the other prayers in a pattern they have developed that recognizes the seasonal variety of the prayers.

The new position of the Prayer of Humble Access took the congregation by surprise (in fact they thought the vicar had got it wrong) but now they have realized how appropriate the words are, in both versions, coming immediately before communion.

5 We depart: Living his risen life

After the climax of the service in receiving Holy Communion, there is all too often a temptation to get through the last bit as quickly as possible. Instead, we should try to use this final section of the service as a time for reflection before being sent out into the world to 'live and work to your praise and glory'.

This final section has two elements. The first is to use the notes in the texts to good effect.

> *Silence is kept.*
>
> *The post communion or another suitable prayer is said.*
>
> *All may say one of these prayers*
>
> *All* **Almighty God,**
> **We thank you for feeding us . . .**
>
> *(or)*
>
> *All* **Father of all,**
> **we give you thanks and praise . . .**

So there are three distinct sections of prayer following communion.

• The first is corporate silence. The same principles apply here as I mentioned in connection with the Collect at the start of the service. The silence should not be missed out, even if the service is running late, but it is important that the clergy or other leaders of worship do not use a congregational silence as a chance to do something else, like cleaning the chalice or checking the next hymn. The clergy should sit down for a few moments and use the chance themselves to reflect on the grace of God granted through Holy Communion.

- There follows the Post Communion. This is a presidential prayer, and is probably best said by a single voice. *Calendar, Lectionary and Collects* provides a Post Communion for each Sunday and Holy Day. These, like the collects, are strongly seasonal but do not relate to the readings of the three-year cycle. They usually contain some reference to Holy Communion.

  Other post communion prayers may be found in *Enriching the Christian Year*. Those in the second (thematic) half of the book are especially useful.

- The third distinct prayer is for congregational use. *Common Worship* retains the two prayers from the ASB for after communion.

All **Almighty God,**
   we thank you for feeding us . . .

(or)

All **Father of all,**
   we give you thanks and praise . . .

Either of these may be used and both are suggested as congregational prayers. The fine prayer 'Father of all . . .' may not be appropriate for use by the whole congregation. It is a long and involved prayer that was written to be said by a single voice. Such prayers do not always lend themselves to congregational use.

There are also four alternative prayers in the Supplementary Texts (pp. 297–8). These pick up on some of the different themes in Holy Communion and might be used to provide seasonal variety or to emphasize one of these themes (see Chapter 7, 'The Defining Image').

The second element of the period after communion is the Dismissal. This begins after the post communion prayers and changes the focus of the worshippers towards the world. This is as significant as the Gathering and should not be seen in simply functional terms.

When I worked in an inner city parish in Nottingham the parish priest used to say:

> Next week's service will begin with the coffee after this week's service!

His point was that living the gospel, refreshed and inspired by hearing the word and receiving communion, is integral to our worship. Indeed, worship that does not 'send us out in the power of your Spirit to live and work' is missing a vital ingredient.

The brief section after communion should not, therefore, be hurried through to the sound of people making coffee and a steaming urn at the back of the church.

A hymn may be sung

The ordering of the final part of the service is something that needs to be given careful thought. The practical question is 'Where does the final hymn go?'

Common Worship is clear that it comes before the Blessing and Dismissal, and this is logical because there is little point in being blessed, told to go home and then proceeding to sing again. However, the tradition of a big final hymn to process out to will die hard in many places. Whatever solution is adopted, clear symbolism should take precedence over what the choir wants to do!

The Blessing

The default setting for the Blessing is the familiar text: 'The peace of God . . .' and this is provided in the main text of *Common Worship* Order One. However, alternatives are provided on page 299 and each set of Seasonal Provisions (except for Maundy Thursday) provides an additional seasonal blessing. Most of these texts are familiar from the ASB.

An option which has grown in favour in recent years has been the Solemn Blessing for use at Principal Feasts and Holy Days (see *Enriching the Christian Year*). This takes a Trinitarian form in three sentences, each with reference to one person of the Trinity and followed by an Amen, before the final Trinitarian blessing.

Dismissal

Three texts for the Dismissal are provided. The first two, 'Go in peace to love and serve the Lord' and 'Go in the peace of Christ', are the same as in the ASB. However, the third marks a very slight change. For Easter the ASB simply gave instruction to add 'Alleluia, Alleluia' to the end of both versicle and response. *Common Worship* prints both versicle and response:

---

or, from Easter Day to Pentecost

Go in the peace of Christ. Alleluia, Alleluia.
All **Thanks be to God. Alleluia, Alleluia.**

In this way it avoids the confusion over whether to drop the Amen before the Alleluias!

The dismissal at **St Matthew's** makes slight changes to the order laid down in *Common Worship*. Following communion, a short silence is kept during which the president sits in the chair behind the altar. After the silence he or she prays the Post Communion and then announces the final hymn. During the hymn the deacon washes the vessels.

At the end of the hymn the congregation joins together in saying one of the prayers in the main text, which is then followed by the Blessing. At this point the parish notices and banns of marriage are read, followed by the Dismissal, said by the person acting as deacon, and the procession of servers, choir and clergy to the back of the church.

At **St Mark's** the vessels are cleaned during the hymns and songs that have been sung during communion. There follows a period of silence before the Post Communion from CLC and the material from *Common Worship* is used as in the main text. The president says the Blessing and the Dismissal.

The consecrated bread and wine that is not required for communion at **St Luke's** is placed on a side table after communion to be consumed following the service. When communion is over and the selection of hymns and songs that accompanied the distribution has been completed, the Post Communion is said by the whole congregation (mirroring their use of the Collect). The Worship Team recognizes that there are occasions when the prayer does not lend itself to being said by the whole congregation and therefore uses a single voice when appropriate.

The format of the service after the communion at **St John's** is as laid out in the text of *Common Worship*.

A simple check-list

As ministers prepare to lead any service, they need to know that they will have all the texts at their fingertips, both those that will be said alone and those that the congregation will join in. Here is a simple check-list which will ensure that as the leader of worship you are never caught out!

Part of Service	Which form?	Text
Form of Preparation		
Prayers of Penitence		
Collect + Introduction		
Prayers of Intercession		
Introduction to the Peace		
Table Prayers		
Eucharistic Prayer		
Breaking of the Bread		
Invitation to Communion		
Prayer after Communion		
Blessing		

6 Order Two

As I discussed in Chapter 1, *Common Worship* provides two different forms for the Holy Communion. Order One, as we have already seen, broadly follows the ASB Rite A, while Order Two follows the order of *The Book of Common Prayer* 'as commonly used'.

'As commonly used' is a recognition that the BCP order for Holy Communion is seldom used as it is printed in the book. Instead, a variety of changes are often made locally. These include:

- omitting the Ten Commandments, or using the Summary of the Law;

- omitting the Prayer for the Sovereign;

- using a responsive form of the Prayer for the Church Militant;

- omitting the exhortations;

- adding the Agnus Dei.

There are also some minor textual changes that are often made:

- In the Prayer for the Church Militant the BCP has 'that they may truly and *indifferently* minister justice' while the 'customary variation' has 'that they may truly and *impartially* minister justice'.

One change that has not been made in *Common Worship* Order Two is the use of the word 'property' in the Prayer of Humble Access. Here we have an interesting example of how the use of language changes. Some ministers choose to change the word 'property' to 'nature', as in the contemporary version of the text. However, since the arrival of computers and especially Windows 95, the word 'property' is now more easily understood in the sense in which the Prayer Book uses it.

Provision for a modern-language text of the Prayer Book shape was also made in the ASB, as 'The Order following the pattern of the Book of Common Prayer' (p. 146). This followed on from the intercession of Rite A. However, this provision has not been very widely used.

Traditional language

Order Two offers 'the Prayer Book as used' in two forms. First, in traditional language, with a few minor changes from *The Book of Common Prayer* as listed below.

- The Summary of the Law and Kyries are printed in the main text as alternatives to the Ten Commandments.

- The Collect may be introduced with 'The Lord be with you'. This greeting may also be used at the start of the Sursum Corda.

- After the Gospel is announced the congregation may reply 'Glory be to thee, O Lord', with a similar reply following the reading.

- Only four offertory sentences are printed but others may be used.

- Provision is made for biddings prior to the Prayers of Intercession.

- The Benedictus may be added to the end of the Sanctus.

- A note allows the shape of the Prayer of Consecration to be similar to that of Order One (Prayers of Consecration and Oblation followed by the Lord's Prayer).

- A note says that the proper prefaces in the Supplementary Texts may be used in Order Two.

- The Agnus Dei may be used.

Contemporary language

In the contemporary language form, the shape of the rite is the same as the traditional order; however, some additional variety is made to the texts noted above.

- Greater freedom is allowed for in the introduction to the Collect (as in Order One).

- Prayers of Intercession follow Order One form (the Church, creation, human society, the sovereign and those in authority, the local community, those who suffer and the communion of saints).

- Two texts for the Confession are printed as options. The first is a contemporary version of the BCP prayer, while the second is 'Father eternal, giver of light and grace' from the ASB (p. 166) and *Common Worship* Supplementary Texts.

- Two prayers after communion are provided: first, the Prayer of Oblation from the BCP and second, 'Father of all, we give you thanks and praise', from the ASB (p. 144).

- However, it should be noted that there is no provision in Order Two in Contemporary Language for the Sursum Corda to start with 'The Lord be with you' nor for the Agnus Dei to be used.

There is one new text in this version, as a short exhortation prior to the invitation to Confession (the exhortation is also found in the Form of Preparation for Order One).

Brothers and sisters in Christ,
as we gather at the Lord's table
we must recall the promises and warnings
  given to us in the Scriptures.
Let us therefore examine ourselves and repent of our sins.
Let us give thanks to God
  for his redemption of the world through his Son Jesus
  Christ,
and as we remember Christ's death for us,
and receive this pledge of his love,
let us resolve to serve him in holiness and righteousness
all the days of our life.

It is hoped that Order Two will be seen as a viable alternative to Order One in places where *The Book of Common Prayer* has been regularly used. Indeed, there is no reason why Order Two should not be used in churches that are unfamiliar with the Prayer Book language.

> For example, of our four pen-picture churches, **St Matthew's** uses Order Two in Contemporary Language (BCP shape and modern language) at the 8 a.m. Holy Communion, making a sensible link, in contemporary language, between the new texts for the service and the use of the new lectionary provision in *Calendar, Lectionary and Collects*.
>
> At **St John's** use is made of Order Two (BCP shape and language) at the monthly 'BCP' celebration, because the Worship Committee thinks that it is easier to follow the text straight through rather than jump around in the BCP. Order Two does give the opportunity for the Prayer Book shape for the Holy Communion to be more accessible in worship.

As Jeremy Fletcher comments in his introduction to this book: 'Time will tell if the inclusion of these services in the *Common Worship* main volume will introduce them to a new set of worshippers and mark a revival of their use!'

7 The defining image

What is this Holy Communion which this book is about? That question might have been asked at the outset rather than at the end. However, having explored many of the options open to us in the way in which we celebrate this central act of Christian worship, we are now in a position to ask the more basic questions. Having looked at the practicalities we are led to ask more.

I have called this chapter 'The Defining Image' because it is the image that we have of the service that will determine not only what we call it but also how we plan, prepare for and enact this worship which is so central to the majority of Christian people. It is the defining image.

The 'defining image' can be described in terms of the deeply held views of worshippers. We have all heard some of the items in the following list given as the only understanding that there can be of the Holy Communion.

- *The private communion of one person with their creator.* The 'early service', a time when the faithful make their personal journey to the altar rail and receive the body and blood of their saviour.

- *A homely gathering of like-minded people.* Here the focus is on the fellowship of 'the Lord's people at the Lord's table on the Lord's day'. The Parish Communion movement and liturgical reform have restored a primitive understanding of Holy Communion as a fellowship meal. The president now faces the congregation, a greater sense of community has been built up by exchanging the Peace and a new orientation towards mission is found in the closing sections of the service. All this has brought a new sense of meeting with each other as well as meeting with God.

- *The Messianic Banquet, a foretaste of the banquet in heaven in which the faithful will share.* In some settings, clouds of incense and highly ornate churches are designedly reminiscent of the visions of heaven recorded in the Bible. Worship in these churches is often highly ritualized, leading to an emphasis on the future hope of the worshipper. We might see this image as a vertical one, which emphasizes participation in that banquet.

- *The 'outward and visible sign of an inward and spiritual grace'*. The words of the Catechism which suggest that the Holy Communion is primarily one of the means by which we are fed by God for the journey of life.

- *The road to Emmaus*. The Holy Communion as the place where we can meet with Jesus in a focused way as he reveals himself to us in the breaking of the bread.

- *The Lord's Supper*. The thankful remembering of the last meal that Jesus had with his disciples and, in remembering, obeying the command to 'do this in memory of me'. This is what Wesley called the 'converting and confirming ordinance' and the 'sacrament of becoming'.

- *Breaking the word and the bread*. Placing equal emphasis on opening up the word of God by reading Scripture and preaching, and the breaking and sharing of the bread.

- *A radical meal*. A sharing of simple things, bread and wine, in the context of the approaching death of Jesus or the celebration of the fulfilment of the prophecy in Isaiah 61: 'he has sent me to bring good news to the oppressed, to bind up the broken-hearted, to proclaim liberty to the captives, and release to the prisoners'.

These are just a few of the images that can be used to describe the service in which we all participate. However, none of them can be said to be the only interpretation of what we are doing. On the contrary, each service will contain elements of several of these images and those participating will have different understandings of what it is they are doing.

The significance of the 'defining image' for this book is that it will become the fulcrum for many of the choices that have to be made about the shape, language and content of each celebration. The basic texts used will remain the same, providing the common core to *Common Worship*, but the supporting texts will be very different, depending upon the theological position taken.

Admittedly there are other important factors, such as season, the presence of children and the resources available to the worship leader or president. However, for many of the choices the key issue will be 'What kind of gathering are we planning for?'

Deeper strands

Underlying each of these defining images are two deeper strands, which are fundamental to our understanding of what we are doing when we 'make eucharist' and which contribute in different measure to each 'defining image'.

Growth

The Greek theological notion of *theosis*, in which the individual journeys on pilgrimage towards perfection, makes the point that we cannot remain in one place. To do so is to atrophy and ultimately to die, both spiritually and physically. Growth is fundamental to our understanding of Holy Communion: it is, after all, a meal.

Many churches now have a mission statement, expressing, in a short and pithy way, the self-understanding of a congregation. Often they include such ideas as 'to grow in the faith and love of God' or some similar phrase. Thus growth is seen as essential in the Christian life.

But I wonder how this element of a mission statement is applied to worship. Often, I suggest, another line in the statement will be applied to worship, while worship as a vehicle for growth is sidelined. The thinking of the Liturgical Commission on the three parts of Holy Communion (Gathering, Transformation and Mission) suggests that if we do not expect change and growth to take place in the lives of worshippers then a vital ingredient is missing from that worship.

Gathering	Word	Sacrament	Dismissal
The coming together of the people of God	Listen Respond Affirm	Take Bless Break Give	Go in peace to love and serve the Lord
From the world, bringing the business of the week into the presence of God	The promises of God heard in the light of our own experience	At the table the food of God is received	Nourished by word and sacrament to be Christ in the world
	Transformation		

The table above shows the transforming flow of the service from gathering to departing. Each of the 'defining images' will result in a different emphasis in each of the boxes. For example, in the 'Messianic banquet' image, the focus will be on the table. If, on the other hand, the emphasis is on 'the Lord's people on the Lord's day', then the focus will be on the gathering of the people of God in worship.

In each of the 'images', however, there is an element of bringing with us from the world our joys and our sadnesses, our hopes and our fears. These experiences are rightly placed before God in our worship and no more obviously so than in Holy Communion. As Jeremy Fletcher says in his introduction, 'Simply put, we should not leave the place of worship as the same people who entered it.'

Mission

The table above also reveals the significance of mission in eucharistic worship. To say week by week or even day by day, 'send us out . . .', might be another place in which familiarity with liturgical texts can lead to contempt. But if we do not go from the gathering of God's faithful people into his world with a renewed sense of mission, then we have surely failed to recognize the transforming power of the sacrament in our lives.

As our theology of Holy Communion is formed by our 'defining image', so too will be the mission that flows from it. We are, after all, seeking to recruit people into the celebration of Holy Communion as the heart of their newly found Christian discipleship.

If we allow ourselves to be unresponsive to the call of Jesus to 'make disciples' we will only have half heard the command, 'do this in memory of me'.

Each of these defining images and the deeper strands will have an impact on the way in which we plan and prepare for eucharistic worship.

PART 2
Pastoral and practical concerns

8 Music

Many clergy will have been confronted by the irate parishioner who claims after the service that

> 'We didn't know any of those hymns. Who on earth chose them?'

In some ways the complaint is quite valid. Familiar music certainly does enable a sense of worship to be developed within the eucharistic setting. However, it is also true that many congregations could do with an element of challenge in their hymn singing. To use only 1–333 in *Hymns Ancient and Modern New Standard* or hymns written before 1930, as many in our congregations would prefer, robs us of hymns of great beauty and powerful meaning. Indeed, many modern worship songs have a directness and personal approach that are not found in hymns of older origin. Let us not forget, however, that of the 770 hymns in the standard version of *Hymns Ancient and Modern* (the 1916 edition), very few are now sung regularly. The editorial axe has fallen on many old hymns and will doubtless fall on a similar, or even higher, percentage of modern songs.

One solution to the unknown hymn syndrome is to take a few minutes before the service to teach a new hymn or song to the congregation. However, it is equally unwise to introduce too much new musical material to a congregation at one go! As with so much of what has been said, the key is careful planning for the introduction of new material.

There are other questions associated with the singing of hymns or songs. The authors of *Sing His Glory*, a book of hymn and song selections based on the Church's year, make the following points in their preface:

> many people absorb their theology from, and are nurtured in the faith by, the words which they sing, and the tunes to which they sing those words.

And

> Hymns need to be appropriate to the points at which they
> are sung . . . This ought to be obvious, but it is still
> possible to find churches where the congregation is invited
> to sing 'O enter then his gates with praise' just as it is
> about to go home. (*Sing His Glory*, Canterbury Press,
> 1997, p. vii)

So once again we find that at the heart of our worship is careful
planning and the making of appropriate choices for the particular
setting, either of season, place or time. If the authors of *Sing His
Glory* are right, and I think that they are, then here we have a
great chance to influence the emphasis of the service we are
planning.

Sing psalms and hymns and spiritual songs

Hymn choosing that is done by one person sitting at a desk with
a great pile of hymnbooks is unlikely to produce the best effect.
Instead, a team of people representing those who will be leading
worship, the musicians and, for goodness' sake, somebody from
the congregation would be a more collaborative way of working
and provide a more balanced diet.

There are many places to which this group or, if absolutely
necessary, the organist or priest can turn for help in the task. A
full list of these resources may be found on page 115.

He who sings prays twice

The five conventional slots for hymns or songs in the Holy
Communion do not by any means include all the opportunities
for music. First there are other points in the service where a song
might be appropriate. Congregational settings for the Holy
Communion are widely used but songs and hymns can provide a
more singable alternative.

For example:

- A hymn or song in the place of the Gloria.

- A musical response can be used during the Prayers of

Intercession. For example, the responsive chants of the Taizé or Iona communities provide simple and memorable musical responses. It is important to work out with the musicians involved how they will know when to start playing. A simple cue phrase works well:

Leader: Let us pray to the Lord . . .
Musical introduction . . .
All sing

- 'Holy, Holy, Holy is the Lord' in place of the Sanctus and, using the same tune, 'Jesus, Jesus, Jesus is the Lord' as the memorial acclamation ('Christ has died . . .') and 'Worthy, Worthy, Worthy is the Lord' (or 'Glory . . .') at the end of the prayer as a concluding act of praise.

- 'We break this bread to share in the body of Christ' at the breaking of the bread.

- Another example is *The Twenty-First Century Hymn Book* (Kevin Mayhew, 1999), which offers a selection of settings for the Gloria, Sanctus and Agnus Dei to modern and familiar tunes, which might be used in an informal service. (For example, the Gloria set to 'An English Country Garden' or 'The Ash Grove', or the Sanctus set to Slane or, again, 'The Ash Grove'.)

These are just a few examples, but the new eucharistic prayers offer a great deal of scope for using hymns or songs as congregational responses. Used in this way, the musicians might play the melody quietly during the prayer so as to enable the congregation to come in at the right point. An example of this, using the words of the traditional texts, is *The Shalom Setting* by John Harding, published by St John's College, Nottingham.

The examples given have all been from a modern idiom; however, this need not be the case, as traditional music also lends itself to this use.

Prayer F offers the possibility of using the plainsong, chant
'Rejoice, rejoice, Emmanuel . . .':

The Lord is here.
All **His Spirit is with us.**

Lift up your hearts.
All **We lift them to the Lord.**

Let us give thanks to the Lord our God.
All **It is right to give thanks and praise.**

You are worthy of our thanks and praise   Musicians begin
Lord God of truth . . .   to play the
As we watch for the signs of your   Plainsong melody
   kingdom on earth,
we echo the song of the angels in heaven,
evermore praising you and *saying*:

All **Holy, holy, holy Lord,**   The Sanctus may
   God of power and might,   be said or sung,
   heaven and earth are full of your or might be
    glory.   replaced with the
   Hosanna in the highest.   refrain as below.
   [Blessed is he who comes in the
   name of the Lord.
   Hosanna in the highest.]

Lord God, you are the most holy one,   Plainsong melody
enthroned in splendour and light,   restarted, the
yet in the coming of your Son Jesus Christ   refrain 'Rejoice,
you reveal the power of your love   rejoice,
made perfect in our human weakness.   Emmanuel . . .' is
                                                 sung.

[Rejoice,
Rejoice, Emmanuel shall come to thee, O Israel.]

Embracing our humanity,
Jesus showed us the way of salvation . . .
As we recall the one, perfect sacrifice of our redemption,
Father, by your Holy Spirit let these gifts of your creation
be to us the body and blood of our Lord Jesus Christ;

form us into the likeness of Christ
and make us a perfect offering in your sight.

[Rejoice,
Rejoice, Emmanuel shall come to thee, O Israel.]

The use of music during the Eucharistic Prayer need not be confined to the prayers which offer responses. The quiet playing of the organ or appropriately chosen recorded music may be used in all the prayers as the presiding minister speaks the words of the prayer.

Music in quiet places

Just as hymns and songs can be used in a variety of places, so music should not be seen only as a cover for some action that has no words. Indeed, there are many places in which music can be used to enhance the action, once the decision has been taken that music is not simply to fill in when nothing else is happening.

For example, in many churches quiet organ music is played as the preacher goes to the pulpit. Developing this theme, a meditative piece of orchestral music (played over a PA system), following the sermon or in the middle of a dramatic reading of the Gospel, can focus the thoughts of worshippers most effectively.

Not just the organ

It might seem from many Anglican churches that the organ has to be the only instrument heard in worship. Historically, however, there is a great tradition of small bands leading singing in the churches of England before the organ took over! Many churches have a wealth of untapped musical talent which could be used to great effect in a small band to lead worship.

As with many of the issues connected with the planning of worship, we do best in the area of music if we have a balanced diet. Some hymns and songs lend themselves to accompaniment by a group consisting of a piano, flute and oboe, for example. To make things easier, modern hymn and song selections are often published with parts for a variety of instruments.

The best is yet to come

At this early stage in the process of renewing the services of the Church, there has been little music written especially for the new texts. However, there is a very wide range of possibilities for music in the new services and we can be sure that musicians will take advantage of this. It is likely that over the next few years music will be composed to fill this gap.

9 Children

The presence of children at Holy Communion provides us with a number of challenges. These challenges are derived from the principle that has become increasingly popular in recent years:

> Children are not only the future of the church, they are also its present.

The most far-reaching of these challenges will be for those churches who decide that children may be admitted to Holy Communion on the basis of their baptism and prior to confirmation. However, the issues, although different, are just as important for those who decide that confirmation is the point at which a person should be admitted to communion.

The issues are:

- How can we present the liturgy of both word and sacrament in such a way that children may participate fully?

- How do we ensure that by providing for the presence of children we do not exclude adults?

And perhaps most significantly:

- Is all-age worship possible in a eucharistic context?

I suggest that one solution to all these issues lies in the way in which a church creates a balanced diet of worship and nurture for all its members. If this single issue is placed high on the agenda of the church, then the result will be a place in which all people can grow in the knowledge and love of God and find ways to express that in worship.

So this chapter will be concerned not only with making the church a place where children want to be, but also ensuring that their grandparents want to be there too!

A variety of models

There are a variety of different ways of addressing this issue.

Children should be seen but not heard

A crèche and Sunday school operate in a separate building every week. Children are taken straight there and collected by their parents as they go home. The material used is of good quality and the children do learn Bible stories and about how to be a Christian. But the rest of the church is unaware of their existence and therefore robbed of the chance to enjoy youthful enthusiasm and the freshness of approach that children often bring to the discovery of faith. Some will defend this by saying that the devotions of those gathered for worship should not be disturbed. I do not share this view!

Children in the Way

The title of a Church report published some years ago neatly sums up the view of some churches. The church recognizes that children are indeed a part of the 'Way', but on an emotional level it feels that children get in the way. One solution to this might be to have an additional, non-eucharistic service on a Sunday morning after the Parish Communion, which is focused on children and newcomers. While this might appear to kill two birds with one stone, it has the danger of fragmenting the parish family, newcomers will not meet the existing congregation and adults will not be aware of the presence of children in the church.

We are all children of the same heavenly Father

Children arrive at church with their parents but leave for their Liturgy of the Word in the church hall, which is adjacent to the church, after the opening hymn and greeting. The material used in Junior Church is split into appropriate age groups and follows the readings used in church. On one Sunday a month the children may return at the Peace, while on the other three a longer time is spent in Junior Church so that the leaders can go into more depth on a particular subject. The choice is made on the basis of the material.

In this model, careful thought must be given to those parts of the service in which children will participate. For example:

- members of the Junior Church might form the procession of the gifts at the Preparation of the Table;

- one of the responsive eucharistic prayers might be used;

- on occasions children could be invited to gather round the altar for the Eucharistic Prayer;

- the children's work in Junior Church should always be shown to the congregation; the insights of children shown through art and drama, or simply by asking them what they have done in Junior Church, will often shed new light on the passages that have been considered by the adult congregation.

You will guess that this is the option that I favour, not because the other two do not have real advantages to bring to the life of the church, and may in some places be the right way to address the issue, but because my own feeling is that baptized children, as full members of the church, need the spiritual nourishment provided by receiving communion and that the way in which their church organizes this is very significant.

All-age worship

A diet simply made up of what in our family we call 'nursery food' is unlikely to satisfy all tastes for very long. The same is true of worship. All-age worship can enable people of all ages to gather in worship and grow in faith. However, this requires a high level of preparation and planning. Celebrating Holy Communion as an all-age service is possible but adds to the need for creativity and planning. Below are some questions to ask in your planning team, which can help in this process.

➤ How many different voices will be heard during the service?

➤ Do all the congregation know enough of the songs? (There is no point in having songs that the children know but that leave the other members of the congregation as spectators. This might become a performance instead of congregational worship.)

> Are you including simple and memorable texts which non-readers can know by heart?

> Are any responses simple enough for the young people present to join in?

> Does the proposed talk or address 'dumb down' the Bible reading? If the answer is yes, then change it. It is quite possible to explain something in terms that will be comprehensible to all while not doubting the intelligence of any.

Taking these points into account will help to create an act of worship in which all may participate and grow spiritually.

Resources

There are now a bewildering number of books for children's work in churches. For many people the choice will be simple: just carry on using what we have used for ages. However, not all material is as good or comprehensive as the rest and it is worth looking at some of the material available or consulting your Diocesan Children's Adviser on the choice that will suit your situation best. Some of the materials also provide resources for adult groups and the main service in church.

Let the children come to me

As a parent of a three year old, I know how distracting she can be to other members of the congregation. Equally, I know how embarrassing it can be to have a young child with you in church. But I also know that my daughter will enter into the worship of the church if she is allowed to, at her own level. If she becomes aware of others tutting at her she will feel excluded and consequently make all the more noise.

The weekly pew leaflet in our church says:

> Children are welcome in this church.
> Please let them worship God in their own way.

10 Making the change

For many readers the hardest question will be: 'How do I make the change from the ASB to *Common Worship*?' However, this need not be too daunting a prospect. The material is really very similar, and apart from the few pitfalls that I have pointed out, the change should be relatively straightforward.

The initial change to *Common Worship* is not the only one that you will face. Having once learnt to use the flexibility of *Common Worship*, it will be possible to continue to explore its wealth of provision. It may also lead to a more fundamental look at how your church conducts its worship.

A debate in the PCC

The final decision about which services and options to use will be made by the incumbent and PCC. For many Church Councils this will involve some education about the issues raised in making choices about worship. A good start will be a preliminary discussion which raises the issues about why there is a need to change and what the new services offer. A member of your Diocesan Liturgical Committee or Diocesan Worship Group might introduce this discussion.

Decision one

The first thing to decide is 'Who is going to decide?' The final decision must be made by the PCC, but a small Worship Committee or Worship Planning Group will probably make the best job of the preparatory work of examining the texts and making the choices.

This group should probably consist of:

- clergy and those who lead worship

- musicians

- children's workers

- a churchwarden

- two or three PCC members.

This group could continue to have a role in the planning of worship after the change to *Common Worship* has been made.

The task

The task is not complicated and below is a list of some of the points to be remembered.

Preparation

- When the Worship Committee has been appointed, give all the members of the group a copy of the texts and this book! This may sound obvious, but if they have had a chance to read the material before meeting, the task will be much simpler.

- Draw up a list of all the occasions for which the group is going to plan the use of *Common Worship*.

- Look at what you use currently. This will help you to get a picture of where what you do now works well and where your services might be improved. It will also help to ensure that the group understands the basic structure of the Holy Communion service.

- Focus especially on the new texts. These include the eucharistic prayers, penitential material and the various parts of the Supplementary Texts.

Making the choices

- Which version of the service will we use for each occasion?

  ➤ Order One in traditional or contemporary language

  ➤ Order Two in traditional or contemporary language

- Will we use the same version on Sundays and weekdays, for a quiet 8 a.m. service and for the main worship on Sundays?

- Which of the options will we use?

  ➤ For the Preparation

  ➤ For the Confession

  ➤ How will we arrange the Prayers of Intercession?

  ➤ How will we decide which Eucharistic Prayer to use?

- How shall we use seasonal material?

Presenting the texts

- How will we present the text?

  ➤ Buy the book (published by Church House Publishing and available from Church House Bookshop, 31 Great Smith Street, London SW1P 3BN).

  ➤ Produce one 'home-grown edition' that covers all the eventualities.

  ➤ Produce a series of seasonal booklets.

- If we opt for seasonal booklets, how do we decide which seasonal material to use?

  ➤ This is a year's task. The Worship Planning Group should begin working on a seasonal booklet several months in advance. All the material, from all appropriate sources, should be gathered together and a decision made as to which most closely fits the needs of your congregation.

  ➤ You should also buy a copy of Mark Earey's very helpful book, *Producing Your Own Orders of Service* (CHP/*Praxis*, 2000).

- Other questions include:

  ➤ What will be our default settings? These are the options that we normally use.

➤ Will we use the Collect for Purity?

➤ Where will the Penitential material go?

➤ Will we use the Prayer of Humble Access? If so, in which version?

How do we introduce all this to the congregations?

In many ways this will be the most significant part of the process. Regular worshippers have become familiar with a set of texts and will want to know why they have to change, even if these changes are not very great. The following section will help you to make this change and to adopt *Common Worship*.

A time to teach and a time to learn

This change to *Common Worship* Holy Communion, although a much smaller step than with some other parts of *Common Worship*, deserves to be taken seriously. It is the chance for congregations to look not only at what they do and how they do it, but also to spend time learning about this service. As the central act of worship in many churches, Holy Communion receives surprisingly little teaching from the pulpit or in house groups. Below are some ideas as to how this might be done.

Sermon series

I suggest a short series of three sermons as follows:

1 The Liturgy of the Word

2 The Liturgy of the Sacrament

3 An 'exploded Holy Communion'. In place of a sermon, a series of short commentaries on the text and the action of the Holy Communion. This would be most appropriate on the Sunday on which *Common Worship* is introduced.

Point in the service	Commentary on
a) **After the greeting**	Gathering, Confession and the Collect
b) **After the Collect**	Liturgy of the Word and responses in Creed and Intercession
c) **Before the Peace**	Peace, Preparation of the Table, the Eucharistic Prayer, Prayer of Humble Access and Communion, The Prayer after Communion.
d) **Before the blessing**	The Blessing and Dismissal

House group material

Many basic courses in Christianity omit reference to Holy Communion entirely. One exception to this is *Emmaus*, which does provide later in the material a short course on worship which includes Holy Communion. Making the change to *Common Worship* gives an excellent opportunity to produce some material for house groups or occasional groups meeting in Lent or Advent. This book is not the right place to provide a complete course on the subject; however, here are some session headings and notes that might be developed into a full course.

Session 1: What is worship?

Looking at some biblical texts
Psalm 100
Luke 1.46–55

Session 2: The shape of Holy Communion

Introducing the four sections
The shape of the Liturgy of the Word
The shape of the Liturgy of the Sacrament

Session 3: Gathering to hear the word

How can we listen effectively?
How do we respond to the word?

Session 4: Gathering to feed on God

1 Corinthians 11.23ff.

Session 5: Go in peace to love and serve the Lord

Growth
Mission

Life-long liturgical learning

The process of changing over to *Common Worship* will not end when all your services of Holy Communion use the new materials, nor should we relax from the process of liturgical education just because the change has been made.

For *Common Worship* to live and flourish in our parishes, we will need to provide regular opportunities for members of our congregations to engage with the texts and review the choices that have been made.

The world of adult training and education speaks of 'life-long learning'; perhaps liturgy might be a subject for life-long learning too!

11 Some resources

In this chapter I offer a selection of resources that are available to accompany the use of *Common Worship*. In each section there are new books and resources coming on the market all the time, as authors and composers use the new services for the first time.

Calendar, Lectionary and Collects

B. David Hostetter, *Prayers for the Seasons of God's People*, Abingdon, 1997.
Very useful selection including Prayer of the Day, Prayer of Thanksgiving. Not authorized for use but nevertheless a useful resource.

Martin Kitchen, Georgiana Heskins and Stephen Motyer, *Word of Promise* (Year A, 1998); *Word of Truth* (Year B, 1999); *Word of Life* (Year C, 1997), Canterbury Press.
A devotional guide to the Principal Service Lectionary of CLC.

Opening Prayers, Canterbury Press, 1999.
ICEL Collects.

Michael Perham, *Celebrate the Christian Story*, SPCK, 1997.
A useful guide to the background of the *Calendar, Lectionary and Collects* of *Common Worship*.

Sharon Swain, *Bible Sentences for Common Worship*, SPCK, 1998.
Provides opening sentences for each Sunday and for themes and seasons.

Brother Tristam SSF, *The Word of the Lord*, Canterbury Press, 1998.
The full text of CLC readings for all three years.

Michael Vasey et al., *Introducing the New Lectionary*, Grove Books, 1996 (Worship Series No. 141).

Jonathan Priestland Young, *Enriching the Liturgy*, SPCK, 1998. Prayers and sentences for the new lectionary. This provides an introductory sentence, Gospel Acclamations and Table Prayers for a variety of occasions, but is not clearly laid out.

Using the Psalms

There is a variety of ways of singing psalms (see Chapter 3). Here are some musical settings:

Psalms and Music for the Eucharist, McCrimmon, 1998.

Psalms for the Church Choir and Music Group, Kevin Mayhew, 1997. Indexed for CLC and ASB, the Psalms are by number rather than by Sunday use.

Psalm Songs, Cassell, 1998.
Three volumes of songs based on the Psalms: Advent and Christmas; Lent, Holy Week and Easter; and Ordinary Time.

Sunday Psalms, Kevin Mayhew, 1998.
All 150 psalms and a liturgical calendar.

Keeping saints' days

Robert Atwell (ed.), *Celebrating the Saints*, Canterbury Press, 1998. Daily spiritual readings for the saints' days of *Calendar, Lectionary and Collects*.

Robert Atwell, *Celebrating the Seasons*, Canterbury Press, 1999. Daily readings from a variety of sources old and new.

Eleanor and Rachel Sayers, *Following in Their Steps*, Kevin Mayhew, 1997.
Short biographies of the saints in CLC. These might be used as a short homily at a mid-week Communion service.

Brother Tristam SSF, *Exciting Holiness*, Canterbury Press, 1997. Readings, collects and post communion prayers for the saints of *Calendar, Lectionary and Collects*.

Leading intercessions

David Adam, *Traces of Glory*, SPCK, 1999.

Raymond Chapman, *Prayers for Sundays, Holy Days and Festivals*, Canterbury Press.

John Pritchard, *The Intercessions Handbook*, SPCK, 1997.
This is a very full book offering texts for prayers, hints on how to organize the Prayers of Intercession and some ideas for developing the intercession slot in worship.

Susan Sayers, *Living Stones*, Kevin Mayhew, Year A: 1998; Year B: 1999; Year C: 1997.

Books of prayers

John Blakesley, *Garland of Faith*, Gracewing, 1998.
Medieval prayers for the three-year lectionary.

Ted Burge, *Lord for All Seasons*, Canterbury Press, 1998.
Meditative prayers on the lectionary.

Collects and Post Communions in Traditional Language, CHP, 1999.
The collects and post communions of *Calendar, Lectionary and Collects* in traditional language for use with the traditional language texts of *Common Worship*.

Choosing hymns and songs

The following resources provide ideas for the Principal Service in the *Common Worship* lectionary.

- The Royal School of Church Music publishes *Sunday by Sunday: a weekly guide for those who plan worship*. This provides a selection of hymns from most of the well-known hymnbooks and collections of modern worship songs, indexed in such a way as to provide help with an appropriate point in the service for a particular hymn or song. Suggestions are also provided for anthems suited to a variety of musical capabilities, ideas for organ music before and after the service and some suggestions about singing the psalm. It also includes articles about various aspects of worship and some new songs.

Sunday by Sunday is available to Friends or Affiliates from RSCM Cleveland Lodge, Westhumble, Dorking, Surrey, RH5 6BW.

- Both the *New English Hymnal* and *Hymns Ancient and Modern New Standard* have published an index for use with the *Common Worship* lectionary.

- *Sing His Glory* (Canterbury Press, 1997) is a guide to hymn-choosing which provides a table of hymns suitable for the Principal Service for each Sunday of the three-year cycle. It also makes suggestions as to the appropriate point in the service for a hymn. The selection tends to be of older hymns rather than some of the more recent worship songs.

Four computer resources with more to follow . . .

- *Hymn Quest* provides the words for a wide variety of hymns and songs.

- *The Hymns and Songs of Canterbury Press* with the words of *A & M New Standard*, *New English Hymnal* and *English Praise*.

- *Songs of Fellowship* words on disk (comes free with full music copy).

- *Visual Liturgy* (CHP) makes the creation of 'home-grown' orders of service a very much simpler task. Offers suggestions for hymns and songs from a very wide range of sources on a themed basis. What is not provided is a list of music suitable for each Sunday in the lectionary.

New hymnbooks

- *Common Praise*, Canterbury Press, 2000.

- *Sing Glory*, Kevin Mayhew, 1999.
  This has a very useful scriptural index.

Singing the service

The Royal School of Church Music provides settings and music for the Eucharistic Prayer written for use with *Common Worship*.

Resources for children

Ecumenical team, *Partners in Learning*, Methodist Church and NCEC, annual publication in September,
Includes *All Together*, a section for all-age worship and material for four age groups

Leslie Francis and Diana Drayson, *Bread for all the Family*, Gracewing, 1996.
An all-age learning programme based on Holy Communion.

International and ecumenical team, *The Whole People of God*, Canterbury Press, 1999.
Very full set of materials for all age groups and 'Intergenerational work'. Follows Revised Common Lectionary, different in minor ways from CLC. Some material is not authorized for use in the Church of England: for example, texts for Confession, Absolution and Profession of Faith.

Diana Murrie and Hamish Bruce (eds), *Worship Through the Christian Year*, CHP/National Society, Year A: 1998; Year B: 1999; Year C: 1997.

SALT, Scripture Union.
Provides material for children's activities and teaching.

Susan Sayers, *Living Stones*, Kevin Mayhew, Year A: 1998; Year B: 1999; Year C: 1997.
An all-age book of resources for every Sunday of the year. Material for three age groups and suggestions for Prayers of Intercession.

Stuart Thomas, *Come to the Feast*, Kevin Mayhew, Book One: 1997; Book Two: 1998.
Material for festival seasons with ideas for liturgical action,

Index